GET

650.14   Deback, Alan
DEB
         Het Hired in a Tough Market

GET HIRED

in a
Tough Market

INSIDER SECRETS TO FIND AND
LAND THE JOB YOU NEED *NOW*

ALAN DE BACK

New York   Chicago   San Francisco   Lisbon   London   Madrid   Mexico City
Milan   New Delhi   San Juan   Seoul   Singapore   Sydney   Toronto

1 2 3 4 5 6 7 8 9 10 11 12 13 14 15 16 17 18 19 20 21 22 DOC/DOC 0 9

ISBN 978-0-07-163705-3
MHID   0-07-163705-2

Interior design by Think Book Works

McGraw-Hill books are available at special quantity discounts to use as premiums and sales promotions or for use in corporate training programs. To contact a representative, please e-mail us at bulksales@mcgraw-hill.com.

Contents

Preface

Even in the best of times, looking for a new job is a rigorous process. When your search is compounded by a tough market, however, the search becomes even more difficult. The competition increases, job leads are more difficult to find, and it's easy to lose hope. The job hunters who succeed in such markets are the ones who invest the time and effort it *really* takes. They know they must leave no stone unturned and pursue every possible strategy.

As a career counselor and trainer for more than twenty years, I've seen my clients enjoy both wild success and miserable failure. And I'm going to tell you what's responsible for both. I don't find them the jobs . . . I only provide the advice and guidance. The job hunter is the one who must network, pursue the leads, and make things happen!

The job searches I've conducted during my own career have also had varying degrees of success, but I always knew I was the one accountable for the outcome. When I first graduated from college, the economy was in tough shape. I chose not to follow the advice of my college career counselor since I was convinced that I knew best. (What twenty-year-old doesn't think he or she knows best?) I had my stack of résumés printed and pursued the foolproof strategy of randomly mailing them to anyone I could think of. I was convinced that was *the* way to look for a job. Can you guess what happened? I finally accepted a job at minimum wage selling men's shoes in a local department store. I stayed in this position for a year after graduation.

My job search strategies have certainly improved over the years, especially after I became a career counselor and learned the "ins and outs" of a successful job search. Over the years I've found several jobs through my personal and professional networks. I found my first job out of graduate school, however, through an advertisement in the *New York Times*, and I later found another job through the *Washington Post*. So don't let anyone tell you that you can't actually land a job if it has been heavily advertised in a major newspaper. The point is, I expanded my pool of search strategies as I learned more about how the system worked, and although a successful search still required abundant energy and effort, it usually took less time.

The tools at a job hunter's disposal have evolved greatly in recent years, especially with the advent of the Internet. Job listings are easily accessed online, and researching potential employers no longer necessitates a trip to the library. The simple truth remains, however, that a range of approaches is critical and will greatly enhance your search.

I'm excited about sharing what I've learned through the years with you in this book. I've striven to walk you through the process in the very sequence in which you will need to plan and conduct your search. I've also made sure that you have lots of worksheets, templates, checklists, and examples to provide practical guidance and support along the way. These practical resources will illuminate the murkier parts of the process.

You'll also meet Mary and Kevin, and follow them through their job searches. Both characters are based on a compilation of behaviors I've observed in my years as a counselor and trainer. You may find yourself shaking your head over Mary's approach, but everything she does is something I've seen a real client do—and representative of things we all do subconsciously, to a greater or lesser extent. I guarantee you will learn as much from her failures as from Kevin's successes.

These truly are tough times for job seekers. The competition is stiff, and opportunities are limited. But the most important element of the process is always the same—you. You control how much effort and energy you commit to your job search, and picking up this book was the perfect start! I'm convinced that the information and tools in this book will lead you not just to a job but to one you enjoy. Best of luck as you pursue your next big opportunity!

PART 1

Pre-Work: Laying the Foundation for Success Before You Start

Have you ever started out on a car trip to a new destination without a map or global positioning system (GPS)? What was the end result? Unless you have a superior sense of direction, you probably ended up wandering aimlessly. You may have eventually reached your destination several hours late, or perhaps you became discouraged and returned home. In either case, arriving at your destination without some form of directions probably seemed beyond your reach.

A job search without good pre-work and clear targets is very similar to that aimless car trip. You won't have a good knowledge base from which to start the journey, and you will have little idea of the pathway(s) to your goal of employment. Job seekers who don't do some basic pre-work will shortly find themselves wandering aimlessly. They may appear frantic with activity, but activity doesn't necessarily mean progress. They generally take much longer to reach their goal, if they get there at all. Often they end up settling for something quite different from what they really want. You must have a strategic plan identifying your targets in order to reach your job search goal. In a very tight economy, this is an especially critical component of gaining the edge over the competition.

So now that you know that you need a firm foundation and a solid plan of action, how do you go about developing and implementing such a plan? Part 1 of this book is designed to help you develop the foundation from which to launch your search and to provide you with the tools to conduct an effective and targeted search.

WHAT ARE THE BASICS?

Before you establish your foundation and develop your plan, you need to tackle a number of logistical issues related to your job search. Ignoring these issues will sabotage you before you even get started. Here are the questions that you must answer:

How Much Time Should You Devote to Your Search?

The short answer to this question is as much time as you possibly can. We all know, however, that this won't happen. Realistically, how much time can and should you devote? Your personal situation will certainly have some impact. Do you have personal responsibilities (children, elderly parents, etc.) that require major chunks of your time? Are there certain times of day that tend to be quieter than others? You will need to carefully balance these various duties with the time you must devote to your job search.

Some career counselors and coaches will tell you that job searching is now your full-time job and you absolutely must treat it as such. But because job searching can be such a grind, a full forty hours a week may just be too much for you to tolerate and still remain productive. You will need to decide how much time is realistic and then develop a schedule you can stick to. This will be critical to keeping yourself on track. Perhaps all you can tolerate is six hours per day. In that case, many people find that 9:00 to 12:00 A.M., an hour for lunch, and 1:00 to 4:00 P.M. works well. Adhering to those hours each day will ensure that you'll be much more productive than during a longer day that isn't as well defined.

In any case, plan to devote a significant amount of time to your search each and every day. You should also build in some time for leisure reading, a walk around the block, or whatever activity helps you relax. You will be more productive if you include that "downtime" (see the next question).

Finally, give yourself permission to take weekends off. Your family and friends need to see you and get some of your time—and this will help you maintain your sanity. Use the weekends to disengage from the stress of the search and actually have some fun!

How Will You Reward and Take Care of Yourself?

Your ultimate goal, of course, is to find the job you want. It's very likely that this will take substantial time and effort, but your reward will be that fantastic job you land.

As with any long-term goal, you must set milestones for yourself along the way (perhaps as often as weekly). It helps to build a mini-reward system as you reach those milestones. One client rewarded herself with an inexpensive night out at a neighborhood restaurant. Another gave himself a round of golf at a nearby municipal golf course. Choose rewards that work for you, but be sure you actually earn them by reaching your milestones, which might be calling a certain number of contacts, sending out a certain number of résumés, and so on.

As I hinted earlier, your state of mind is also a huge consideration. Job hunting is wearying, and it's easy to become emotionally exhausted. When you do find yourself mentally spent, you tend to spin your wheels in lieu of making real progress. While making a concerted effort, you need to take care of yourself both mentally and physically.

These two aspects of well-being are closely related, and most people find that physical activity positively impacts their mental attitude. In other words, this is not the time to cancel your gym membership. Be sure to build time into your schedule for some sort of physical activity—even if it is a half-hour walk around the block.

Also be sure to actively seek out opportunities to interact with others socially. Some job seekers retreat into isolation. They either may be embarrassed about their situation or find the search process so exhausting that they shut themselves off from friends and family. Social interaction will help to recharge your batteries and improve your mental outlook. This can only help your job search.

Where Will You Work on Your Job Search?

You must have an area in your home that is your "space" to conduct your search. If you already have a home office you're in great shape, as that can automatically become your search space. If you don't, you need to identify where your search space will be. Even if it's just a corner in a bedroom or family room, having a designated space is critical to your success. You and those you live with will treat it as "your" space for the time being.

Once you've identified some suitable space, take the time to set it up properly. Do you have the office supplies that you will need—or is it time for a trip to the office supply store? Is there a computer in this space? How are you going to organize the reams of paper that will probably accompany your search? Do you have some file drawers set up and files to organize all of your job search materials? A space that isn't well organized will impede your progress.

Once your space is set up, make sure that everyone you live with understands the "hands-off" rule. During your search you may need to quickly find some kind of document. If a well-meaning significant other has cleaned or straightened your space, you could lose something important. For anyone who lives with you, the rule must truly be "hands off." You don't want to suffer the fate of one job seeker whose spouse decided to clean up and threw away important documents that ended up costing him a job.

What Should You Tell the People You Live With?

It's a good idea to communicate with your significant other or the people you live with about your plan for your job search.

Many job seekers report that because they are physically around and available more than usual, interruptions make it difficult to focus on what they need to accomplish. You should communicate your weekly time line and overall strategies so that everyone around you understands them. Also communicate when you *will* be available, so that people know when they can grab you. Making sure that the people around you understand your strategy and availability will make your search a whole lot easier.

A job search can be a big strain on a personal relationship with your spouse or significant other. You should definitely have a conversation with that person early on in your search. He or she needs to be assured that you will be doing everything you can to find your next opportunity. After all, your significant other's financial security is probably at stake, which can cause serious concerns. At the same time, you need to help him or her understand that daily nagging or detailed questioning about your progress won't help you to be productive. Too many relationships have been impacted negatively by a job search for you to avoid this important conversation!

To Whom Will You Be Accountable?

The short answer, of course, is that you will be accountable to yourself, but many job seekers also find it helpful to enlist a friend or colleague to be their "job search buddy." This doesn't need to be someone who is an expert in the job search process, but it should be someone you trust to give you honest feedback about your progress. Your buddy shouldn't be someone who is too close to you, such as your spouse or significant other. The relationship is too intimate for such a person to be objective, and putting him or her in that position could quickly undermine your relationship.

Once you've identified someone and that person has agreed to be your job search buddy, set up a regular check-in time with him or her. It's best to do it weekly, and in person. Many job seekers find it easiest to talk over a cup of coffee. Use the time to review what you have accomplished in the past week and then discuss what you plan for the coming week. Be sure that your buddy is someone who will give you honest feedback and take you to task if you aren't doing what you have committed to. Although you will, of course, hold yourself accountable in this process, having a job search buddy gives you accountability to someone else too—which can make the crucial difference!

Know Where You're Going

Developing Your Job Search Plan with Self-Assessments

You must know yourself and what you have to offer to a potential employer before you actively pursue any opportunities. In times of tough competition, too many job hunters immediately jump into the search without considering what it is they have to sell. It's inefficient to market yourself without having any idea of the strengths or skills that make you the ideal "product" for an employer to hire. You will have an advantage over your competition and make yourself far more attractive to a potential employer by identifying your unique skill sets and what distinguishes you from others. You must take the time and effort to figure out what makes you stand out from the crowd!

In this chapter, we'll review a process for thoroughly examining your skill sets. You'll learn how to identify your strongest skills and how to articulate them effectively. You'll also have an opportunity to examine your interests and how they relate to your skill sets. Combining your interests and skills will increase your motivation and make you a stronger candidate—always important, but especially critical in a tough job market.

MARY ATTENDS A RECEPTION

Mary had been invited to attend a reception for a friend who was retiring. She generally hated attending events like this, but she had known the colleague for many years and wanted to honor her achievements. *Besides,* she thought to herself, *most of the people at the reception will be people who work in my field. Who knows what kinds of contacts I might make?*

Mary arrived at the reception and began to mingle. She noticed a small group of friends she hadn't seen recently and joined them. They introduced her to Sarah, another woman chatting with the group.

After a few minutes, Mary found herself in a conversation with Sarah. As they discussed their work, Sarah mentioned an upcoming job opening with her organization. *Wow,* thought Mary, *maybe I've struck gold here!*

"So what type of opening do you have coming up?" asked Mary. "I may be looking for a new opportunity."

"Well," answered Sarah, "it's a project manager position working with one of our most critical clients. We really need to find someone with the right skill set who will also be a good fit with this client. What are some of your skills in project management?"

Mary was shocked. She hadn't expected to be asked about her skills and hadn't really thought them through. "Well," she started, "I'm awfully good with people. I like people and people really seem to like me. That's all I can really think of at the moment."

"Oh," answered Sarah. "Well, people skills are a small but important piece of the puzzle, for sure."

Within a few moments, Sarah had politely excused herself and moved on to chat with another group. Mary was left with her glass of wine and her thoughts. *I think she wanted to know more about what skills I could bring to her organization,* she thought, *but people skills were all that I could come up with.*

WHY ARE SKILLS IMPORTANT?

Mary's experience is just one example of why knowing yourself is the first critical step in the job search process. In a tough job market, you must take every advantage to set yourself apart from the competition. A major component of that process is knowing your skill sets cold and being ready to articulate those clearly and concisely. Most employers are looking for new employees who will be able to hit the ground running and begin contributing, in a significant way, as quickly as possible. In current work environments, which have often been cut to the bone, there just isn't time to hand-hold new employees and to slowly bring them up to speed. If you aren't seen as someone who possesses the skills needed to become productive quickly, your competition will win out.

You *must* know who you are and what your skills are in order to make that case for yourself.

Mary has clearly not reflected on her strongest skill sets and how she has used them. In fact, she's not unusual—most of us never make the effort to identify our various skill sets. Sure, there are things that you know you do well in both your personal and work lives, but in your day-to-day life you are rarely asked to describe them. The job search process, on the other hand, puts you in a variety of situations where you need to be able to identify and describe those skills on demand. If you do the homework, you'll be ready. If you don't, you'll find yourself in the same shoes as the bulk of your competition—struggling with how to sell yourself and your skills.

Most skills can be categorized as either *technical* skills or *transferable* skills. You need to assess both types of skills. Here are short definitions of each:

○ **Technical skills:** These are skills that relate to a specific technical competency. Examples might be proficiency with computer software programs, fluency in a foreign language, or the ability to use a certain type of mechanical equipment.

○ **Transferable skills:** These are skills that have to do with how you interact with or communicate with other people. Examples could be presentation skills, supervisory skills, or writing skills. Transferable skills are also sometimes called "soft" skills because they are needed in a variety of work environments in a range of career fields.

Most career fields require a mixture of technical and transferable skills in order to achieve competency. Many people find it easier to recognize and communicate their technical skills. The transferable skills tend to be hidden or taken for granted. You must make the effort to identify and describe both skill sets.

By now, you probably understand the need to better recognize exactly what your skills are, but where do you begin? How do you determine exactly what your skills are—especially your more subtle transferable skills?

HOW DO YOU IDENTIFY YOUR SKILLS?

To develop a solid overall view of both your technical and transferable skills will require quite a bit of work and introspection. You will probably need to go outside yourself to get input from others. The end result, however, will be well worth the effort. This easy-to-follow three-step process will help you, as will the accompanying worksheets.

1. **Write two success stories.** Using Worksheet 1.1 at the end of this chapter, write two stories that describe some sort of achievement or success you have experienced. One should be

strictly work-related, and the other can come from either work or your personal life (perhaps related to volunteer work you have done or an activity in an organization you belong to). As you write your stories, describe what you did, what obstacles got in the way and how you overcame them, and what strengths you drew upon to ultimately achieve your end result or goal.

After you have written your stories, read through them several times. Let a few hours (or even days) lapse between reviews. The breaks will give you the opportunity to really think through your achievements and what went into them. You may recall additional information that you want to add as a result of your reviews. Highlight any skills (technical or transferable) that you actually mentioned in your stories and then identify other skills you may have used in the course of each example.

2. **Read your current job description (and past job descriptions, if available).** Most of us review our job descriptions only at the time we are hired for a job or if the fundamentals of the job are changed. Using a highlighter, review your current (and past) job descriptions. In most job descriptions, specific skills will be clearly identified. Mark those skills with your highlighter and read through them again. Are there other skills you can identify that are important to the responsibilities outlined? Note those skills as you identify them. Be sure to focus on *both* technical and transferable skills. As you did when you reviewed your success/achievement stories, allow a few hours or days to lapse and read the job descriptions again looking for any skills you may have missed in your initial review.

3. **Seek input from your coworkers and friends.** Despite your best efforts to look inside yourself, your coworkers and friends will see you differently. They will probably be able to identify skills that you don't even realize you possess. Coworkers will be able to zero in on skills they have observed at work; friends should be able to identify skills you've exhibited in your personal life (often transferable skills). Have a conversation with several coworkers and friends you trust.

Ask them to think about both technical and transferable skills. Can they cite concrete examples of how you've displayed the skills they identify?

After you've gone through the three-step process, make a comprehensive list of your skills. Use Worksheet 1.2 to divide those skills into technical skills and transferable skills. You will probably have many skills identified in each category.

To make the list more useful, you need to pare down your large list of skills. Think about the strength of each of the skills you've identified, and then categorize them by placing a check mark in the "A" column for your strongest skills, a check mark in the "B" column for your second tier of skills, and a check mark in the "C" column for your least proficient skills.

HOW DO YOU KNOW WHICH SKILLS ARE IMPORTANT?

You've completed the skills identification exercises and have identified your skill sets and prioritized them. Now what? How will you use this list? Even with your skills arranged in priority order, your list is probably still somewhat long and cumbersome.

First, you need to consider what skills are important to you. What skills do you most enjoy using? Then you'll need to research what skills are in demand for the career field in which you want to work. Finally, you'll look for the crossover between the skills you're most interested in and those that are in demand. Here's how you can do it.

What Are Your Preferred Skills?

Starting with your "A" skills, examine your list. Which skills involve activities you actually enjoy doing? For example, suppose that one "A" skill is review of complex commercial contracts. Although this is one of your primary skills, perhaps you've been doing it for years and you're tired of it. That's probably not a skill you want to promote in searching for your next job. Instead, let's say you also have a strong skill in *negotiating* contracts and you really enjoy that part. That is a skill you may want to emphasize. Use a highlighter to examine your "A" skills and identify the ones that you would really like to use in your next job.

What Skills Are in Demand?

Your preferred skills are meaningless if employers aren't looking for them. The next step is to determine what skills are important for the kinds of jobs for which you will be applying and interviewing. What exactly are potential employers looking for?

Use online job listings or newspaper ads to find job descriptions for the types of positions you are looking for. Read the descriptions carefully and highlight the skills that are described. Also, search for skills that are implied in the responsibilities that are described. Go back to your list of skills and highlight with a different color your "A" skills found in the job descriptions you've read. These are the skills that are in demand by employers in your field.

How Do You Align Your Preferences with Skills in Demand?

When you look at your lists of preferred "A" skills and your in-demand "A" skills, is there any crossover? Typically, at least a few of your "A" skills will be included in both lists. These are the skills you need to promote during your job search. They will provide you with job satisfaction in the workplace and will also be attractive to potential employers in your field. A job using these skill sets will be a win-win for both you and your employer!

If you're not seeing enough crossover, go back and complete the same process with your "B" skills that you just completed with your "A" skills. Although your "B" skills are not your ultimate strengths, they are still areas where you have competencies that you can promote.

You've now aligned your skill preferences with the skills in demand in your field and have your skills "short list." These are the skills that will most effectively market you to potential employers. You'll want to highlight these skills in the "one-minute commercial" that you'll develop in the next chapter. You'll also want to be sure to emphasize these skills in your résumé. Most of your competition will not go through this detailed skills identification process, so the fact that you have done so will give you a definite edge in a tough job market.

WHAT ABOUT YOUR INTERESTS?

Although not all interests relate directly to possible job or career options, an opportunity that includes areas in which you have a personal interest will certainly be more enjoyable, and enjoyment of your work generally correlates with more success and greater longevity at your new position. You should certainly take into consideration what your interests are. You may also find it valuable to compare your interests to your prioritized skill lists and investigate which skills you use when pursuing your personal interests. Those skill sets can be valuable in ways you may not even have considered.

To help you think about your interests, and which of them might be applicable in your career field, take a few moments to complete Worksheet 1.3. This worksheet will help you identify those interests you find most enjoyable.

SHOULD YOU CONSIDER YOUR VALUES AT WORK?

Your personal values are critical to how happy you are at work. If you are doing work that isn't aligned with your values or you work for a company whose values oppose those you find important, you'll find yourself frustrated and potentially very dissatisfied—which doesn't bode well for your success at that organization. Considering your values and how they relate in the workplace is critical.

Spend a little time checking off the values on Worksheet 1.4 that you believe are important. Then use the "Top 10" section of this worksheet to choose the values that are most important to you. As you pursue your job search, keep your values list handy. Are the jobs you are applying for and the employers they involve in alignment with your most important values? Many employers will provide their core values on their websites, which should make your job easier. Be sure to review them as part of your employer research before an interview.

Look at Kevin's story as an example of an effective way to promote your skills and values when opportunities present themselves.

KEVIN ATTENDS A COMMUNITY ASSOCIATION MEETING

Kevin decided to attend the annual meeting of his community association. He had always been active in his community and enjoyed the annual association meeting. Because the meeting was accompanied by a reception, he also liked the opportunity to reconnect with neighbors and friends he hadn't seen in a while.

After the meeting concluded and the reception began, Kevin spotted a group of neighbors he hadn't spoken with for a few months. He joined the group and was soon introduced to a new neighbor, John. After a few minutes of conversation with John, Kevin discovered that they both worked in the same career field. John asked for more details about Kevin's experience. Kevin replied with a quick overview of the type of work he had done, mentioning a couple of primary skills. Then he mentioned how he had helped customers with their problems and gave a short, specific example. He did not mention at this point that he was job hunting but continued an interesting conversation about common issues that he and John had faced in serving their customers.

As Kevin drove home from the meeting, he reflected on his conversations. He had enjoyed renewing acquaintances with several of his neighbors. The highlight, however, was meeting John. They had similar backgrounds and experiences and had had a great conversation about some of the mutual customer challenges they had faced. *I really need to keep in touch with John,* thought Kevin.

———————————————————○———————————————————

WORKSHEET 1.1 \ *Your Success Story*

What did you do?

What were the obstacles?

How did you overcome the obstacles?

What were the results/outcomes?

WORKSHEET 1.1   CONTINUED

What did you do?

What were the obstacles?

How did you overcome the obstacles?

What were the results/outcomes?

WORKSHEET 1.2 | *Your Skills List*

SKILL	TECHNICAL SKILL?	TRANSFERABLE SKILL?	A	B	C

WORKSHEET 1.3   *Your Interests*

The most satisfying work will include skills and activities that match your personal interests. Code each of the following interests as to how much you like or dislike them.

1 Like very much
2 Like somewhat
3 Neutral
4 Dislike somewhat
5 Dislike very much

_____ Fixing things   _____ Helping others

_____ Public speaking   _____ Teaching

_____ Solving mathematical problems   _____ Researching

_____ Discussing/debating   _____ Leading others

_____ Keeping detailed records   _____ Thinking/meditating

_____ Building things   _____ Solving mechanical problems

_____ Listening to people/problems   _____ Playing or listening to music

_____ Organizing things   _____ Designing things

_____ Writing fiction   _____ Writing nonfiction

_____ Reading   _____ Planning events

_____ Selling things   _____ Exercising

_____ Cooking

WORKSHEET 1.4 \ *Your Workplace Values*

Finding a job that matches your personal values to values in the workplace is important to your happiness and success. Review the values in the categories listed below. Check off the ones that are important to you. Use the worksheet on the final page to identify your "Top 10" workplace values.

Work Atmosphere	**Work Substance**
_____ Stability	_____ Originality
_____ Flexibility	_____ Leadership
_____ Fast pace	_____ Risk
_____ Organization	_____ Preciseness
_____ Deadline pressure	_____ Detail orientation
_____ Security	_____ Variety
_____ Steadiness	_____ Creativity
_____ Structure	_____ Inventiveness
_____ Convenient location	_____ Excellence
_____ Calm environment	_____ Variety
_____ Fairness	_____ Growth opportunity
_____ Collaboration	_____ Thoroughness
_____ Pleasant surroundings	_____ Control
_____ Predictability	

Relationships at Work	Fundamental Values
_____ Trust	_____ Power
_____ Thoughtfulness	_____ Integrity
_____ Caring	_____ Capability
_____ Cooperation	_____ Prestige
_____ Competition	_____ Adventure
_____ Teamwork	_____ Status
_____ Independence	_____ Respect
_____ Open-mindedness	_____ Ambition
_____ Harmony	_____ Authenticity
_____ Open communication	_____ Patience
_____ Autonomy	_____ Responsibility
_____ Tolerance	_____ Influence
_____ Loyalty	_____ Self-confidence
	_____ Helping
	_____ Equality
	_____ Achieving
	_____ Contributing

WORKSHEET 1.4 CONTINUED

What Are Your "Top 10" Workplace Values?

1. _____

_____

_____

_____

_____

2. _____

_____

_____

_____

_____

3. _____

_____

_____

_____

_____

4. _____

_____

5. _____

6. _____

7. _____

WORKSHEET 1.4   CONTINUED

8. _____

_____

_____

_____

_____

_____

9. _____

_____

_____

_____

_____

10. _____

_____

_____

_____

_____

Positioning Yourself

Your One-Minute Commercial

Picture yourself at a meeting of a professional association, or perhaps, at a reception where you encounter someone who works in your career field. You are meeting that person for the first time. He or she wants to know about you and what you do. You've identified your primary skill sets, but how do you convey them, and your background, in a way that will pique that person's interest? And how do you make your story concise and memorable?

Alternatively, imagine you are in an interview for the ideal job. Your interviewer asks some variation of the frequently used "Tell me about yourself." You know that the interviewer wants to hear about what you can bring to the organization that will allow you to hit the ground running and be of immediate benefit, but how do you frame your answer? The interview time is limited, and this is going to be a big, important part of the first impression you make on the interviewer.

The answer to both of those situations (and many others) is to prepare and practice an effective one-minute commercial. You'll have a concise, market-sensitive overview of who you are that you can use in a variety of settings. Let's look at how Mary handles this situation.

MARY'S INTERVIEW

Mary walked into the human resources office at an organization where she really wanted to work. By networking with a friend who worked for the company, she had landed an interview for a job for which she believed she had the ideal qualifications. Mary was sure she had done everything right to prepare for the interview. She had researched the company, bought a new interview suit, practiced several standard interview questions, and thought long and hard about how she would sell herself for this job. She was definitely ready for this interview!

After a short wait, Mary was introduced to Todd, the recruiter who would be conducting the interview. Todd smiled widely and seemed very cordial. Mary was pleased by his demeanor and had high hopes for the interview. After they settled into their chairs, Todd began the interview process.

Todd's first question was "Mary, tell me a little bit about yourself."

What kind of interview question is this? Mary wondered. *What in the world does he want to know about me?* After panicking for a few seconds, Mary began to formulate her answer.

"Well," she said, "I was born in a very small town in rural Pennsylvania." She continued for more than five minutes, providing a biography of her life. By the time she finished, Todd was no longer smiling. The interview continued, but the atmosphere had changed.

As Mary left the interview, she didn't have a good feeling about how things had gone. The dynamics had changed after that first question. *I wonder what it is that Todd really wanted to hear?* she wondered.

HOW DO YOU PREPARE A ONE-MINUTE COMMERCIAL?

One of the best ways to be prepared for these and other situations is to develop a "one-minute commercial." Your one-minute commercial provides an organized, concise overview of who you are and what you have to offer. Anyone listening to you can easily understand your primary skill sets and what you have to offer. They'll remember what you said, both because of the content and the way you said it. But how do you put an effective one-minute commercial together?

To develop an effective one-minute commercial, consider this format:

○ **How do you describe who you are and what you do?** Describe what you do using a job title that will have meaning to almost anyone you meet. Your specific organizational job title may be so technical that it is meaningless outside of your workplace. Many job titles also have little relationship to the actual content of the job that you do. Think about what you actually do from day to day, and how you would explain it to someone not in your industry. Develop a descriptive title that captures the essence of what it is that you do.

  You should be able to describe the content of your work in a way that virtually anyone can understand. Someone you meet for the first time will probably not know or understand the acronyms and lingo that you use in your workplace. Every organization tends to have its own "language" that is readily understood by everyone within the organization but means nothing to outsiders. This terminology creeps into your vocabulary subconsciously but is useless to outsiders. Your one-minute commercial needs to be free of such language.

○ **How do you serve your customers?** Most organizations strive to be very customer-focused. After all, customers are what keep the organization alive and thriving. Your focus on customer service is particularly important in a tough economy where organizations are trying to fend off competitors and maintain their customer base. Describe briefly some of the primary types of customers you work with and how you serve them.

  If your customers are primarily internal, focus on how your service makes them more productive. We sometimes don't consider our internal customers to be "real" customers, but they are. What you provide to your internal customers can have a direct impact on organizational results.

In serving your customers, what primary skills do you use? Which are technical and which are transferable? Elaborating on how your skill sets solve customer problems will show that you are customer-focused rather than inwardly focused. Many candidates for jobs become so focused on themselves that they forget how their skills impact their customers. Your focus on customers in your one-minute commercial will give you the edge over your competition.

○ **How are you helping your customers solve their problems?** In a tight job market, the ability to address and solve problems (especially those of your customers) is critical. Most organizations are very interested in hiring effective problem solvers. What are some common customer issues or problems that you face, and how do you work with your customers to solve them? Once again, what primary skill sets do you use?

○ **What is one recent success story?** Although you've identified some primary skill sets and made clear your customer focus, you still haven't described any results. By sharing a brief overview of one recent customer success story, you show that you're the real deal. Not only do you convey a solid understanding of your skills and the importance of using them to benefit your customers, but you have a real-life example to show how you did so. Describing a success lends immediate credibility to your one-minute commercial.

Consider developing a few different one-minute commercials. One might be about your technical skills and the other about transferable skills. That way, you have a couple of options, and you can choose which one to use depending on the situation. Use Worksheet 2.1, provided at the end of this chapter, to develop two different one-minute commercials.

PUTTING IT TOGETHER: AN EXAMPLE OF AN EFFECTIVE ONE-MINUTE COMMERCIAL

Here is a recent example of a one-minute commercial that I developed with a client. As you review this one-minute commercial, try to identify the key components discussed above:

> I am a trainer in the computer industry. I develop and provide training related to the various kinds of computer software that my customers use in their organizations. I work with my customers to fully understand their needs and design customized software training to address those needs. Many of my customers need training for employees with limited computer proficiency, and I make sure that the training I deliver is targeted directly at their level and needs. For example, last month a client needed spreadsheet training for a group of administrative assistants who were experienced only with word processing. I designed training appropriate for their level of knowledge and adapted the tasks that they needed to learn to perform. The client called me two weeks ago to tell me that every one of the people I trained is now productively using spreadsheets for a variety of tasks.

WHAT IS IMPORTANT, OTHER THAN WHAT YOU SAY?

Although you may have developed a great one-minute commercial, it's not just the content that is critical. How you present the content is equally important. Does your communications package reflect someone who is confident and enthused or someone who lacks self-assurance and is just going through the motions?

We'll examine the importance of both voice/tone and body language in greater depth in the chapters about interviewing, but there are some basics that are important to consider when presenting your one-minute commercial.

Voice/Tone

Your voice needs to sound strong and be loud enough to be easily heard. If you are naturally soft-spoken, this may require some practice. A voice that is soft or difficult to hear can be interpreted as reflecting a lack of confidence, even if that isn't that case. After all, perception is reality.

Also important is your tone and inflection. Your tone should show enthusiasm for what you are conveying about yourself. If you have a natural monotone, you will want to practice adding some inflection and enthusiasm to what you say in your one-minute commercial.

Body Language

Your body language also needs to display self-confidence and enthusiasm. From your posture (especially standing at a networking event) to your hand gestures and eye contact, your body language can make or break the success of your one-minute commercial. If you have the opportunity to be videotaped—perhaps by a spouse or friend—that's a great way to be sure that your entire communications package reflects the image you want to present.

HOW DO YOU FINALIZE YOUR ONE-MINUTE COMMERCIAL?

Once you have completed a draft of a one-minute commercial that you believe is effective, share it with friends, coworkers, and anyone whose opinion you respect. Ask for their honest feedback. You will often find that pieces you thought were crystal clear actually aren't. Perhaps you have underemphasized a skill or accomplishment. This feedback will be valuable, so be open to it. Expect to revise your one-minute commercial several times based on the feedback you receive.

After you are comfortable with the content, you will need to practice your one-minute commercial. Many people are self-conscious about talking in front of a mirror, so they only practice silently, thinking that the presentation will come together when the time is appropriate. The problem with this approach is that they've never felt the words cross their lips or heard the words come out of their mouth. The result is often something that sounds very garbled or tentative the first several times—and that can be an opportunity killer.

A better approach is to practice out loud, preferably in front of someone you trust to give you honest feedback. You will actually feel and hear the words, and you'll identify changes that make your commercial much more comfortable to share. You'll sound more fluid and natural.

The goal is not to sound like you're delivering a practiced speech, however counterintuitive that may sound! Instead, you want a commercial that sounds just like natural conversation. When you practice, think about your normal speech patterns and the normal tone of your voice. Ask your observer whether this truly sounds like you, and make changes if it doesn't. Then practice, practice, practice . . . until your commercial flows off your tongue clearly and naturally.

Let's take a look at how Kevin handles the interview situation.

KEVIN'S INTERVIEW

Kevin also had an interview scheduled with Todd. He felt that he was the ideal candidate for the job and really wanted to work for this particular company. He had researched the company, bought a new suit, and practiced some standard questions. He had also gone through some skills assessment exercises to identify his important technical and transferable skills, and he had built a couple of one-minute commercials around various key skills and practiced them until he was very comfortable with them and could repeat them naturally. Kevin was convinced that he was ready to ace this interview.

Kevin arrived at Todd's office, where he was introduced. His first impression of Todd was positive, as Todd cheerfully greeted him and tried to make him comfortable.

As the interview began, Todd asked Kevin the same opening question that he used with almost all candidates: "So, tell me a little bit about yourself." Kevin was well prepared for this question, since it is a common interview opener.

Within about one minute, Kevin outlined a few of his strongest skills (making sure they were tied to the description of the job for which he was interviewing), mentioned how he was using them to serve his customers, and shared a recent success story that used one of the skills. He was pleased when Todd asked a follow-up question about the specifics of how he had met the needs of the very difficult customer.

When Kevin finished answering the follow-up question, Todd flashed a big smile. "Great," he said, "let's continue the interview." *Great,* thought Kevin, *this is off to a very good start.* His confidence bolstered, the discussion with Todd continued. Kevin left the interview feeling very encouraged about his chances and pleased with his performance.

———————————————————○———————————————————

Your one-minute commercial will be a critical part of your job search strategy. We'll explore in future chapters how you can use it in a variety of networking and job search situations. Be sure that it is carefully crafted and effectively practiced to ensure that it presents you and your skills in just the way you want to represent yourself to others!

WORKSHEET 2.1 | *One-Minute Commercial Worksheet*

Who are you/what do you do?

How do you serve your customers?

How are you helping customers solve their problems?

What is one recent success?

WORKSHEET 2.1 | CONTINUED

Who are you/what do you do?

How do you serve your customers?

How are you helping customers solve their problems?

What is one recent success?

Planning and Targeting Your Search

I recently left my home in northern Virginia for a client meeting in Washington, D.C. I thought I knew where I was going but realized when I got into the city that I had made a mistake about the location. I had carelessly left my portable GPS sitting at home, so I ended up wandering around for quite a while. I reached my client's office eventually but was almost a half hour late.

Just as my trip without a concrete plan (and backup device!) almost ended in failure, a job search without a plan can also be endless—and certainly circular. In a tough economy, you must come prepared and be spot-on with your job search efforts.

In the previous chapters, we've examined why you must identify and target your skills. We've also developed a plan for articulating and selling your skills effectively using a one-minute commercial. Let's now focus on your plan of attack. Let's see how Mary did it.

MARY PLANS HER SEARCH

Mary was ready to begin her job search. The problem was she really didn't know where to begin. *This is so overwhelming,* she thought. *How do other people get started? Perhaps,* she reasoned, *I should just jump in and start sending out some résumés. I think that I can use my son's computer, and he probably won't mind if I just leave a pile of things on his desk.* Mary quickly scanned one of the online job boards, selected a couple of positions that looked interesting, and submitted her résumé. *There,* she thought, *that's enough job hunting for one day.*

Over the next couple of weeks, Mary feverishly submitted résumés. She checked several job boards regularly and applied for anything that seemed like a remote possibility. Her frustration grew as she received no responses.

One day, Mary's phone rang.

"Hello," said the caller. "This is Phil Smith from XYZ Industries. Could I please speak with Mary?"

Mary was thrilled. Finally, a response! She spoke with Phil animatedly for the next several minutes. Eventually, Phil asked, "So how would you feel about relocating up here to Nome, Alaska?" *Nome, Alaska!* thought Mary. "Um . . . is that where the position is located?" asked Mary. "Yes," answered Phil. "Didn't you notice the location in the job listing?"

After a couple more minutes, Mary hung up the phone feeling dejected. *I've been applying for everything I could find,* she thought. *I guess I should be paying more attention and concentrating on what are realistic options for me.*

HOW DO YOU PLAN YOUR JOB SEARCH SCHEDULE?

Just as Mary decided to randomly submit some résumés online, many of your job-seeking competitors will be operating without a plan of attack. They won't strategically chart out employers they will contact or how or when that contact will happen. They also won't keep good records of where they've sent résumés, whom they've spoken with, and what transpired. This is dangerous because as you can imagine, it's both personally embarrassing and potentially damaging to receive a call from an employer if you can't remember when or how you first made contact, or what version of your résumé you supplied! You need an effective job search planner to keep track of your contacts and keep your job search moving ahead.

Your job search planner will also be an effective tool to use with your job search buddy. Remember we earlier discussed the importance of a job search buddy to add accountability to your search? Your planner will provide documentation that you and your buddy can review and discuss to ensure that your search is moving ahead on target!

A sample job search planner is included in Worksheet 3.1 at the end of this chapter. You can find similar ones online or even develop your own spreadsheet if you wish. What is important is that you have some sort of planner and rigorous documentation. Most of your competitors won't!

HOW DO YOU PLAN WHERE TO LOOK?

You know that you need to focus on your plan of attack, but how do you get started? A strategic plan that is well thought out is yet another feature that will give you a leg up in a tough economy. A plan will provide you with focus and direction and help you arrive at your ultimate goal faster and more successfully. Despite the temptation to skip this step and dive right in, don't do it. You'll see the payoff in the form of increased focus almost immediately.

Your plan should include several elements that will help narrow your search. Let's take a look at those key elements—and how you can make good decisions about them.

How Do You Research Geographic Areas?

If you are geographically mobile, you should identify regions that will be good targets. Why waste your time on an area where the prospects are slim when another area (even in a tough economy) may provide substantially more opportunities? How do you identify those regions that may be good targets?

- One great resource for overall information about state and metropolitan labor markets is the U.S. Department of Labor Bureau of Labor Statistics. A trip to their website (bls.gov) will give you access to a wide variety of reports. You can quickly determine which state and metropolitan job markets are faring the best overall.
- You may also find that many cities and counties have economic development offices. These offices can provide such information as population statistics, cost of living, major employers and industries, employment trends, and the economic development plans for the specific locale. Most, such as the Economic Development Authority in Fairfax County, Virginia (fairfaxcountyeda.org), have incredibly helpful websites that will give you a great overview of the business climate in the locale.
- To narrow down even further where the jobs are in your particular career field, try to access a job database unique to your field. Most professional associations maintain such databases. When you look at the job listings, some states or metropolitan areas will jump out as centers of opportunity in your field. For help in finding associations related to your field, try the American Society for Association Executives (ASAE) website (asaecenter.org), which includes a comprehensive directory of professional associations.

How Do You Find Out About Specific Industries?

Even during tough economic times, some industries perform better than others. Although you may have expertise in a particular industry, those businesses may not hold the best opportunities for you. The bulk of your professional skills should be transferable to other industries. How can you identify growth industries in general and, more specifically, in the geographic areas you have identified as targets?

○ For an overview of growth industries, read major business publications such as *Forbes, Money*, and *Business Week* on a regular basis. You will quickly identify trends related to major industries. If you can't afford subscriptions to these kinds of publications, you can usually find at least part of the magazine content online at their websites, and most public libraries carry subscriptions to these publications.

○ Our friends at the U.S. Bureau of Labor Statistics publish the *Career Guide to Industries (CGI)*. This guide, available online at bls.gov/oco/cg, provides an overview of dozens of different types of industries, including an overview of expected job prospects.

○ For information about industries in specific geographic areas, a wealth of resources is also available online. Most major metropolitan areas have some sort of local business journal with much of the print edition available online. A quick Internet search will locate such publications for you. You may also find it useful to read the business section from the major daily newspaper(s) in areas you have targeted (which you will almost certainly find online as well). You can quickly develop a working knowledge of the business climate in a given area and a good idea of which industries there provide the greatest opportunities.

What About Specific Companies?

In any recession, some companies are "winners" and some companies are "losers." To some extent, this depends on geography and the industry, but some organizations are just more creative and innovative than others. If you can identify the companies that are "winners" and target your search toward them, your prospects will be greatly enhanced. There are a number of ways to target companies that are succeeding, even in a rough economic environment.

- When you use the variety of business publications described in researching industries, also look for stories highlighting specific companies and organizations. In bad times, to raise morale and to praise success in difficult circumstances, publications seek out and publish stories about organizations that are succeeding. You will probably find some good prospects.
- Local chambers of commerce will frequently provide information about major employers in the area that they cover. For example, the Arlington County, Virginia, Chamber of Commerce maintains an online searchable business directory on their website (arlingtonchamber.org). This is an invaluable resource if you are trying to find particular kinds of businesses or organizations in a specific area!
- Consult the various "Top 100" lists of companies that are published annually by major business magazines such as *Fortune*, *Inc.*, and *Fast Company*. These organizations make the lists because they are doing something right, and that often translates to profits and more job openings. For example, of the companies on *Fortune* magazine's list of "100 Best Companies to Work for 2009," 73 were identified as actively hiring.

What About a Long-Distance Search?

For whatever reason, you may need or want to relocate to a different area. Perhaps the job market is better elsewhere, or perhaps you want to relocate for personal reasons. Whatever the case, you find yourself looking for work long distance. A long-distance search carries with it some unique challenges, and you'll need to strategize carefully how to best use your time and resources. Following are some steps you'll want to consider to make your long-distance search a success.

Inform Everyone in Your Network

Even though the people in your personal and professional networks are probably largely local, you should let all of them know about your search. Ask them if they have any friends, relatives, or colleagues who live in the area where you want to relocate. You'll probably be surprised at the number of people they come up with who might be able to tell you more about the area.

Also make use of your electronic network. In a later chapter we'll examine the use of electronic business and social networking sites. If you belong to any groups, particularly business networking sites like LinkedIn, do a search to see if any members of the group live in the area where you want to relocate. By looking at their profiles, you'll be able to tell how open they are to being contacted. Because you share the interests in the group you both elected to join, that gives you an automatic link.

Contact Professional Associations in the Area

If a professional association you belong to runs a local chapter in the area where you want to relocate, consider making contact with some of the key personnel. People who are actively involved in local chapters tend to be "key players," professionally speaking, in the area where they live and work. They are leaders who will have a good sense of what is happening in the job market and where the upcoming opportunities might be.

One job seeker who wanted to move to an area about one thousand miles from where he lived went to the website of an association he belonged to and found the local chapter for his destination area. He found contact information for each of the chapter officers and e-mailed them all, asking whether they would be willing to have a phone conversation with him about the job market in the area. A couple of the officers ignored his e-mail message, but the majority responded positively and were happy to have a phone conversation with him. He got a couple of good leads—and equally important, he developed professional relationships that continued to yield benefits for years after he moved to the area.

Consider a Trip to the Area

Although there will be time and expense involved, consider a trip to the area where you want to relocate. Get in touch with all of the potential contacts you've developed and let them know you'll be in the area for a few days. Try to set up meetings with as many people as you can. This trip is for business, not pleasure. Schedule several meetings a day while you are in the area, if possible, so that you don't get sidetracked. In fact, don't even go until you have enough meetings set up to make it worth your while.

Long-distance searches have certainly become easier than they were before the advent of the Internet. Now millions of people successfully complete long-distance searches and make moves every year. Just be sure that you are ready for the extra time and effort that a long-distance search entails.

HOW DO YOU PUT IT ALL TOGETHER?

After you've done all your research, you'll want to weave your findings about geographic areas, industries, and specific companies into a workable strategy. This strategy will complement your job search planner and guide you as to where you want to center your search. It will serve as the GPS for your job search.

Worksheet 3.2 will assist you in organizing your job search target strategy information. Be sure that you are realistic as you identify geographic areas, industries, and companies to target. Of course, we'd all like to relocate to Hawaii, but is it realistic?

Let's take a look at how Kevin does with this step.

───────────────○───────────────

KEVIN PLANS HIS SEARCH

Kevin had been through frustrating job hunts in the past and was determined to do it right this time. He knew that rather than jumping right in, he had to do some up-front planning to best utilize his time and resources. He already had a basic résumé that he had received good feedback on, and he knew he'd have to customize it to fit each individual situation. *What sort of preparation do I need to do beyond that?* he asked himself.

The first thing Kevin did was adapt a job search planner to list and record his contacts. He found one online that he felt would fit his needs and made some small changes to it to better match his style. He knew that it would be critical to plan and document his approach of contacts.

After some thought, he also decided to put together a list of options to consider. He came up with the following items that needed to be addressed:

○ Am I open to relocating? If so, to where? How can I research the job market in the areas I would consider?

○ Are there specific industries doing well in this economy? How do I find out which ones they are?

○ What companies (especially in my targeted geographic areas and industries) are hiring? How do I find them?

Kevin knew that this list of questions wasn't complete, but it was a start. He really needed to focus on answering these questions, and others that might come up, in order to maintain focus and momentum in his job search.

───────────────○───────────────

WORKSHEET 3.1   *Job Search Planner*

Date: _____

People I Need to Contact Today

Name/Company   **Phone/E-mail**

_____   _____

_____   _____

_____   _____

_____   _____

_____   _____

People/Companies I Need to Send Résumés Today

Name/Company   **E-mail/Address**

_____   _____

_____   _____

_____   _____

_____   _____

WORKSHEET 3.1

Job Search/Networking/Interview Appointments I Have Today

Name/Company   **Time**

_____   _____

_____   _____

_____   _____

_____   _____

Other Job Search Actions I Need to Take Today

Action   **Person/Company**

_____   _____

_____   _____

_____   _____

Job Search Activities for Future Days

Activity   **Date to Do It**

_____   _____

_____   _____

_____   _____

WORKSHEET 3.2 | *Job Search Target Strategy*

Target Geographic Areas			
Target Industries			
Target Companies			

The Best Marketing Tool Ever

How to Make Your Résumé Relevant

First, repeat the following mantra to yourself three times: "My résumé is *not* an autobiography! My résumé is *not* an autobiography! My résumé is *not* an autobiography!" Many of your job search competitors view their résumés as a comprehensive summary of everything they have ever done in their professional lives. This couldn't be more misguided. Your résumé is your ticket—often the only one—to an interview with a prospective employer. It must be a modern marketing tool, consciously designed to stand out from your many competitors in a tight job market and land you that interview.

How do you make your résumé stand out? You must develop a marketing-oriented résumé that promotes your skills and competencies to a potential employer. As we've discussed already, in a tough economy, employers need people who have the skills to hit the ground running. You must demonstrate through your achievements what you can do to fill an employer's needs. A boring autobiography of everything you have ever done is simply not useful to the person reading it—often a human resources professional with the power to reject it before it even reaches a potential boss.

In this chapter, we'll examine exactly how to build your résumé into a marketing tool. We'll discover what signals an employer to review your résumé in the first place and why you should customize your résumé for every job for which you apply. You'll learn how to best promote yourself in each of the sections of your résumé and also discover what information you should *not* include. Worksheets at the end of the chapter will help you to build the basic structure and content of your résumé as a marketing tool.

Let's see how Mary fares in the résumé process.

MARY'S RÉSUMÉ

As Mary contemplated beginning her job search, she knew that she had to develop a résumé. It had been many years since she had written one, and she remembered how much she hated the process. However, she knew that she couldn't begin her job search without one. With a big sigh, she settled in to begin writing.

Okay, she thought, *the first thing I must do is come up with a good all-purpose objective. It needs to communicate that I'm flexible and can do whatever an employer wants. I also need to make it broad enough so that I won't have to be constantly changing it.* After some contemplation, Mary wrote this as her objective: **Seeking a professional opportunity that will afford me the opportunity to further develop my skills and build my experience.** *That sounds nice and broad,* thought Mary. *Now let me move on to the next section.*

Mary couldn't decide whether the next section should review her education or her work experience. After some thought, she decided on her education. After all, she reasoned, in a tight job market employers will want someone with lots of degrees. Starting with her master's degree, earned in 1981, she carefully listed all of her degrees back to her high school diploma. *There,* she thought, *they can clearly see that I am very well educated.*

Next, Mary reflected on her work experience. She remembered that her experience should be in reverse chronological order and started a list of her responsibilities in each of her previous jobs. As she wrote the description for her most recent job, she strived to be as thorough as possible. *Let's see,* she thought, *I accurately distributed the mail on a daily basis. I also managed the office coffee fund. A lot of my time was spent negotiating contracts, so I should mention that, but I don't think it matters that some of them were worth as much as $15 million. After all, negotiating is negotiating, regardless of the contract value.* After carefully listing every responsibility from each of her past jobs, Mary had already passed the two-page mark with her résumé. *That's okay,* she thought, *they will want a complete picture of everything I've done.*

Finally, Mary considered what other sections should be included in her résumé. *They will want to know that I am stable,* she thought, *so I should mention that I am a homeowner and have lived in the community for twenty-three years. I guess I should also include in my "Personal" section that I have two dogs. Pet lovers are usually good people.*

With that, Mary clicked the "save" key and heaved a great sigh. *That was stressful,* she thought, *but at least the stupid thing is done. I can start sending it out. I won't have to deal with it anymore—I can check it off my list!*

HOW DO YOU GET STARTED?

Knowing that you need to make your résumé a marketing tool, how do you get started? The first step is to reflect on your skill sets and determine how they relate to what employers want in a future employee. Go back to the lists of both technical and transferable skills that you identified in Chapter 1. What were your "A" skills? You'll want to match those skills with the skills in the job description for each job for which you apply. The "matches" should be emphasized in your résumé.

WHAT TYPE OF RÉSUMÉ IS RIGHT FOR YOU?

One résumé type does not fit all. Depending on your background and your level of experience related to the job that you want, one of two different basic résumé types will best fit your needs. Each type has its advantages and drawbacks. In a tough job market, you'll want to carefully consider which type will be most attractive to a prospective employer. We'll carefully examine the basic résumé types, look at the content that goes into each, and consider the best uses of each type. The checklist in Worksheet 4.1 at the end of this chapter will help you to decide which type of résumé is best for your situation.

The Chronological Résumé

The most commonly used type of résumé is the chronological résumé. It's fairly straightforward and reflects your work experience and education in reverse chronological order. Although the format is somewhat autobiographical, you must be sure that your skills stand out, either in a separate section or in the descriptions of your duties at previous jobs. A chronological résumé should not become just an autobiography of everything you have ever done.

The chronological style is preferred by most employers. Because they are accustomed to the format, they tend to be most comfortable with it. They know where to look to find the various pieces of information that they need.

As a job seeker, a chronological résumé will work best if your background is related to the kind of job you are seeking. Your skill sets will usually be directly applicable and your accomplishments focused on areas that will be of interest to a prospective employer. It will be relatively easy for the employer to see how your experience and skills relate. Let's take a look at the various sections of a chronological résumé and what you should include in each.

Heading

Your heading should make it as easy as possible for a potential employer to reach you. A heading that is difficult to read or that includes incomplete information could result in a potential employer not considering you for an opportunity. Although a heading in a very ornate font may look pretty on the computer screen or on paper, it will probably be difficult to read. Believe it or not, a number of résumés will arrive lacking such fundamental information in the heading as a phone number or an e-mail address. A prospective employer will almost certainly move on to the next applicant rather than bother conducting a search for your phone number. Included in your heading should be:

- Your full name
- Your mailing address
- Telephone numbers, including a cellular phone number to provide easy access
- An e-mail address (absolutely required, as many employers find it easiest to e-mail to set up an interview)

Objective

Although having an objective on your résumé used to be mandatory, it is now considered optional. If you do choose to include an objective, it should be specifically targeted to the job for which you are applying. A general, all-purpose objective is meaningless and will work against you, making you appear unfocused.

A good objective should also address what skills and competencies you can provide for a new employer—*not* what it is you want to get from the employer and the new job. Too many objectives, even if they are targeted, don't focus on what the candidate can do for the employer—quite the opposite, in fact.

Summary/Qualifications

Regardless of what you call this section, it should serve as the "headline" for your résumé. Your banner accomplishments or qualities, in terms of what will attract an employer and persuade them to review the rest of your résumé, should go here. You'll provide more detail about these features later in the résumé, but promoting them briefly here can really help attract an employer's attention.

Think about it this way: How do you decide whether or not you will read a newspaper or magazine article? Many of us decide by scanning the headlines and reading those stories that sound interesting. The same goes for the "headline" section of your résumé.

Determining what to include in your "headline" section goes right back to the skills assessment you completed in Chapter 1. What are those skills that you identified both as strengths and as skills in demand for the types of jobs you are applying for? They should be what you highlight in this section. Because many large employers use software packages to scan résumés for keywords and phrases, it's critical that you include in both your Summary/Qualifications and Experience sections the key skills that you identify when you review the job description for the position. These are truly the "hot buttons" that will generate employer interest.

Experience

You need to include the basic information about each of your previous employers (job title, company/organization, city and state, dates employed). You should list your work experience in reverse chronological order, which means starting with your current or most recent experience and working backward. Starting with the current or most recent employer is important because prospective employers will be most interested in what you have accomplished recently. This format provides that information up front.

Rather than simply providing a list of responsibilities in each of your jobs (an autobiographical approach), consider this results-oriented alternative:

○ Provide a one- or two-sentence summary that provides a concise but descriptive overview of what you did in each job.
○ Follow that with a bulleted list that gives examples of your accomplishments/achievements.
○ Start each of your accomplishments with an "action verb" that conveys results.

Employers are looking for results-oriented individuals, and this approach will demonstrate to a potential employer that that's who you are!

Education

Your education should also be listed in reverse chronological order. Once again, a prospective employer will be most interested in your most recent (and/or highest level) degree. You should include the school attended, location, major(s), and degree(s) earned.

References

Many years ago, contact information for references was included at the bottom of a résumé. Recently the trend was for the reference section to simply state "available upon request." Since it is now assumed that you will have a list of references available, there is no longer a need to have a references section on your résumé at all.

The Skills-Based Résumé

A skills-based résumé places the bulk of the attention on your skill sets and minimizes the emphasis on your employment history. It works particularly well for someone trying to change career fields who wants to emphasize the strong skill sets that

What Are the Most Common Résumé Errors?

1. **Incomplete contact information.** It's amazing how many people neglect to include an accurate telephone number or e-mail address. A prospective employer will not take the time to chase you down—they'll simply move on.

2. **Spelling or grammatical errors.** These errors can be summed up in one word: carelessness. If you don't have good quality control in your résumé, what will the quality of your work be like?

3. **False information.** Employers can, and often do, check on whether you actually earned that degree or worked for that company. Résumé fraud has been rampant in recent years, and employers *do* check the facts.

4. **Poor organization.** In a tight job market, employers expect to be able to quickly find the key information they are looking for in your résumé. If it isn't well organized, they'll just move on.

5. **Résumé as autobiography.** Your résumé is a marketing tool. Equal focus on every last aspect of your background will drive prospective employers away. Instead, what is it about you and your background that makes you the best candidate for this particular job?

he or she can bring to the new field. This format also works well for someone who has been out of the workforce for a period of time and wants to de-emphasize the time away and the breaks in employment history. Because the focus is on skill sets, employers see those things first.

The downside of a skills-based résumé is that it may raise a red flag in the mind of a prospective employer. Most employers are used to seeing chronological résumés and may become suspicious that the applicant is trying to hide a spotty work history or something similar if they see any other format. Carefully consider your situation and whether a skills-based résumé will be your best bet. Generally, if you have nothing to hide and are trying to change fields, it may help, especially if technical skills required by the new position are highly valued or rare. However, if you work in a traditional sort of industry, like finance or law, it may be best to stick with the tried and true.

Heading

The format and information included in your heading should be the same as described above in the description of the chronological format: full name, mailing address, telephone numbers (including cellular), e-mail address.

Summary

Most skills-based résumés include a short summary section. This section can be as short as two or three sentences and provides a quick overview of your "hot buttons." You'll probably want to change this section for each job that you apply for in order to ensure that you truly are hitting on the most important elements for this particular job and employer. By identifying and highlighting the two or three skills in your skills/qualifications section that you think will really make the difference for the employer, you're delivering a message that you are a strong candidate. You've given the employer a reason to keep reading and find out more.

Skills/Qualifications

Regardless of what you use as a heading, this is the "meat" of a skills-based résumé. You need to provide an excellent overview of your skills (both technical and transferable) that directly relate to the job or career field. Use the job description for each position for which you apply and match the skills mentioned to your list of "A" skills from Chapter 1.

Avoid the temptation to simply provide a laundry list of skills. Although you may have a long list of excellent skills, if it's *too* long, it will be tedious for employers to sift through and find the skill sets that interest them. Instead, identify a few major categories into which your skills fit and organize them accordingly. Make sure those categories align with the major skill sets in the job description. This will make it much easier for employers to quickly identify the skill sets they want.

Experience

Although skills-based résumés sometimes don't include an experience section, not having one is a big gamble. A résumé that totally lacks an overview of work experience immediately sets off red flags in an employer's head. So *don't* take the risk. Include at least a minimal section outlining your experience.

The experience section in a skills-based résumé is much more brief than in a chronological résumé. Do include the basic information about the employer (job title, company/organization, city and state, dates employed) that would also be in a chronological résumé. Beyond that, just a sentence or two providing a brief overview of what you achieved is sufficient.

Education

This section should follow the same format and guidelines as described for the chronological résumé: schools attended, location, major(s), and degree(s) earned.

References

As with the chronological résumé, there is no need for a references section.

Let's take a look at Kevin's résumé experience.

KEVIN'S RÉSUMÉ

Kevin had just gotten a lead on the perfect job through one of his networking contacts. He knew that he had an ideal background, and the job would be a great next step in his career. He needed a résumé—and fast!

Kevin's first reaction was to dust off his three-year-old résumé, make a couple of updates, and send it off, but he quickly realized that wouldn't be the most effective approach. Instead, he really needed to target his résumé to the opportunity. Since he had a detailed job description for the position, he first read it carefully and highlighted all the skill sets he could identify. Having already gone through the process of identifying his own technical and transferable skills, he could quickly match his skill sets to those outlined in the job description. *This is a good start,* he thought.

Next, Kevin needed to decide which résumé approach to use. Because his experience and skills were directly applicable to the position he was applying for, he decided a traditional chronological format would be best. He also knew, however, that a good summary section would serve as a "headline" for his chronological résumé. He again read the job description, identified three skills that would be real "hot buttons" for this employer, and wrote a concise summary outlining those skills in his experience. *There*, he thought, *this should attract the decision makers' attention and make them want to read the rest of my résumé.*

As he started on the experience section of his résumé, Kevin knew he needed to emphasize results and accomplishments. *In a tight job market, most employers are very concerned about the bottom line,* he reasoned. *They're not interested in a laundry list of my activities but in what I've accomplished and achieved.* Kevin selected a format where he used a sentence or two to describe each of his positions, but then used bulleted statements to outline what his accomplishments had been. Wherever possible he quantified his experience—so that he could provide evidence that he had actually achieved what he claimed.

As Kevin completed the education section of his résumé, he was careful to provide accurate information about each of his degrees in reverse chronological order. Although he knew that it was primarily his experience that would sell him at this point in his career, he wanted to be sure that all of his education was reflected accurately.

After a good deal of effort, Kevin was done with this version of his résumé. He knew that it might be appropriate only for this job, but he also knew that it was well targeted, concise, and easy to read, and it conveyed a sense of achievement and results. Kevin felt confident that in a tight job market his résumé would stand out. The effort he had made would be worthwhile in the end!

The Scannable Résumé

Most organizations have cut their human resources organizations to the bare minimum. This impacts job hunters in a number of ways, including who (or what!) actually reviews your résumé. Even if the organization to which you are applying has a printed copy of your résumé, it's entirely possible that the initial screening won't be done by a person. Instead, it may be done through an electronic scanning process. Regardless of your qualifications, your résumé may or may not make it through this initial process based on a few simple errors. Here are several suggestions to help you make it through this common first step in the screening process:

○ Make use of words from the job description that express the key skills and competencies necessary for the job. The scanner will be looking for those words, and if it doesn't find them, your résumé could be rejected.
○ Use a simple business font such as Arial or Times Roman. A scanner will not recognize a more ornate font. Use at least a 10-point font and preferably a 12-point font.
○ If you are submitting a printed copy of your résumé, print it on white paper. The scanner can more easily "read" text on white paper.

The Electronic Résumé

Many organizations now require that résumés be submitted only through their websites. The advent of this "electronic" résumé poses some issues that could impact how your résumé is received at the other end. Your résumé, in fact, could end up being illegible. You'll need to either convert your résumé into a plain text electronic format or create a résumé without any of the formatting that you would typically use. Either way, you will ensure that your résumé will be clear when it is submitted electronically.

How Do You Create an Electronic Résumé?

○ Don't use any boldfacing, underlining, or italics.

○ If you want to use a bulleted format, use asterisks instead of bullets. Because an asterisk is an actual keyboard symbol, asterisks won't cause issues.

○ Format all text to the left, including the "Heading" section.

How Do You Convert a Standard Résumé?

○ Save a copy of your résumé using "save as," selecting "text only," "ASCII," or "plain text" as the file type. This will remove all the original formatting from the résumé.

○ Review the new version for any errors resulting from removal of the original formatting. You may need to make some changes or corrections.

You'll find a sample of an electronic résumé with the other résumé samples at the end of this chapter.

WHY IS APPEARANCE IMPORTANT?

Like it or not, the appearance of your résumé counts. Whether you are providing a printed copy or submitting online, the appearance of your résumé says a lot about you. Even if you have the best qualifications in the world, a sloppy or poor appearance can cause your résumé to end up in the "no" pile. Here are some important qualities to think about.

Grammar and Spelling

Your résumé is generally the first impression you make. Your first impression should be your best. Poor grammar or misspellings send a message that you lack attention to detail. Use grammar check and spell check for an initial review. Go beyond that, however, and carefully review for additional grammatical or spelling errors. If you aren't confident of your editing, ask a friend or colleague to also review it. Your résumé must be letter-perfect in every way.

Physical Appearance

Your résumé should have a pleasing physical appearance on the page or computer screen. The information should be well organized and easy to find. Leaving adequate white space is critical to a neat and uncluttered appearance. A résumé that is too crowded with information looks overwhelming and makes it harder for employers to find the information that they need.

One Page or More?

The general rule of thumb should be that your résumé never goes more than two pages. One page should be sufficient if you are a recent college graduate or have limited experience. Otherwise, a two-page résumé is perfectly fine. More than two pages *is* too much and often an excuse for an employer to bypass your résumé.

If you do use two pages, a few tips:

○ **Use at least half of the second page.** Having just a few lines at the top of the second page sends a message that you were too lazy to reformat your résumé to fit on one page.
○ **Be sure that the most critical information is on the first page.** If an employer, for some reason, doesn't get to the second page, you want to be sure your most critical selling points are on the first page.
○ **Include some identifying information (at least your name) on the top of the second page, and label it as page two in some way.** Even if your résumé is submitted electronically, it will probably be printed out at some point. The pages can easily become separated and the second page could be lost.

HOW DO YOU PUT IT ALL TOGETHER?

Regardless of what résumé style you choose, expect to spend a substantial amount of time putting it all together and customizing it for every job for which you apply. Most of your competitors won't do either. In a tough economy, this will give you the advantage. Remember that your résumé is usually the first impression a potential employer has of you, and first impressions are lasting. Your résumé won't get you the job, but it will get your foot in the door to sell yourself during the interview process. A carelessly written résumé will quickly be tossed into the proverbial circular file.

This means that you should never think of your résumé as "finished." To truly make a great impression, you must customize it for each opportunity. Read position descriptions carefully to make sure that you include the key skills that an employer is seeking. Failing to include the keywords that describe those skills will quickly eliminate you from the competition. Yes, this customization does take time! In the end, however, the effort will pay off.

To assist you in writing a high-quality, marketing-oriented résumé, two worksheets are included in this chapter. Worksheet 4.2 will help you create a traditional chronological résumé, and Worksheet 4.3 will help you build a skills-based résumé. Use these worksheets to develop the basic framework for your résumé. Concentrate on making it as marketing-oriented as possible and customize it for each employer and position.

Several sample résumés at the end of this chapter will also give you some visuals of each of the various types. Warning!! Don't copy the samples—you *must* modify them to meet your needs in order to sell yourself in the most effective way possible.

Also included near the end of this chapter is a list of action verbs grouped by general skill areas. Use these verbs to describe how you achieved your various accomplishments. They help you appear goal-oriented and self-sufficient.

WHAT ABOUT A COVER LETTER?

You will likely need some form of cover letter to introduce your résumé to an employer. In the old days it was the letter that accompanied your hard copy résumé when the employer opened the envelope. Today it is more likely to be an electronic document that accompanies your electronic résumé, or perhaps the e-mail message that accompanies your résumé. In either case, it should be a concise introduction that will make an employer want to review your résumé. In this section we'll explore a couple of different cover letter formats and discuss the content for each format.

Traditional Format Cover Letter

The traditional cover letter format is typically a brief three-paragraph letter. It introduces your résumé and provides a couple of hot buttons to entice the employer to review your résumé. The traditional format is usually structured something like this:

- **Paragraph one:** Why are you writing? Did someone refer you directly to the employer/position, or did you find a listing on the Internet? If you were referred directly, be sure to mention who referred you and why.
- **Paragraph two:** What are a couple of the hot buttons that make you a great candidate and will make an employer want to review your résumé? Mention a couple of your strongest skills/experiences related to the position using wording something like "as you will see when you review my résumé, . . ." This is the teaser paragraph designed to generate interest.
- **Paragraph three:** This is the thank-you and follow-up paragraph. Thank the employer for their attention to your letter and refer them to the résumé attached. If you intend to do some sort of a follow-up, such as a phone call, indicate

that you will and what your time line for doing so will be. If you say that you will follow up, be sure to do it! Saying that you will follow up and not doing so could be interpreted as a lack of persistence or attention to detail, and could derail your chances for an interview.

Skills-Based Cover Letter

A less traditional cover letter is a skills-based cover letter. The skills-based cover letter directly addresses the major skill sets in the job description and then precisely correlates how your background and experience address each of those skills. This type of cover letter takes far longer to develop and write but can really pique an employer's interest in proceeding to your résumé.

For example, you might address the skill of accuracy by stating that you increased the accuracy of a particular function by X percent. However, you must be certain that this claim is confirmed by the information the employer finds in your résumé.

Regardless of which type of cover letter you use, employ the same attention to detail as with your résumé, and the final product must be totally free of errors. If the job for which you are applying requires excellent writing skills, your cover letter becomes even more important as an example of your writing ability. Some employers will make a decision about whether or not to review a résumé based on the cover letter, so make sure yours shines!

Action Verbs

COMMUNICATION/ PEOPLE SKILLS

Addressed
Advertised
Arbitrated
Arranged
Articulated
Authored
Clarified
Collaborated
Communicated
Composed
Condensed
Conferred
Consulted
Contacted
Conveyed
Convinced
Corresponded
Debated
Defined
Developed
Directed
Discussed
Drafted
Edited
Elicited
Enlisted
Explained
Expressed
Formulated
Furnished
Incorporated
Influenced
Interacted

Interpreted
Interviewed
Involved
Joined
Judged
Lectured
Listened
Marketed
Mediated
Moderated
Negotiated
Observed
Outlined
Participated
Persuaded
Presented
Promoted
Proposed
Publicized
Reconciled
Recruited
Referred
Reinforced
Reported
Resolved
Responded
Solicited
Specified
Spoke
Suggested
Summarized
Synthesized
Translated
Wrote

CREATIVE SKILLS

Acted
Adapted
Began
Combined
Composed
Conceptualized
Condensed
Created
Customized
Designed
Developed
Directed
Displayed
Drew
Entertained
Established
Fashioned
Formulated
Founded
Illustrated
Initiated
Instituted
Integrated
Introduced
Invented
Modeled
Modified
Originated
Performed
Photographed
Planned
Revised
Revitalized

Shaped
Solved

DATA/FINANCIAL SKILLS

Administered
Adjusted
Allocated
Analyzed
Appraised
Assessed
Audited
Balanced
Budgeted
Calculated
Computed
Conserved
Corrected
Determined
Developed
Estimated
Forecasted
Managed
Marketed
Measured
Netted
Planned
Prepared
Programmed
Projected
Qualified
Reconciled
Reduced
Researched
Retrieved

HELPING SKILLS
Adapted
Advocated
Aided
Answered
Arranged
Assessed
Assisted
Clarified
Coached
Collaborated
Contributed
Cooperated
Counseled
Demonstrated
Diagnosed
Educated
Encouraged
Ensured
Expedited
Facilitated
Familiarized
Furthered
Guided
Helped
Intervened
Motivated
Prevented
Provided
Referred
Rehabilitated
Represented
Resolved
Simplified
Supplied
Supported
Volunteered

MANAGEMENT/ LEADERSHIP SKILLS
Administered
Analyzed
Appointed
Approved
Assigned
Attained
Authorized
Chaired
Considered
Consolidated
Contracted
Controlled
Converted
Coordinated
Decided
Delegated
Developed
Directed
Eliminated
Emphasized
Enforced
Enhanced
Established
Executed
Generated
Handled
Headed
Hired
Hosted
Improved
Incorporated
Increased
Initiated
Inspected
Instituted
Led
Managed
Merged
Motivated
Navigated
Organized
Originated
Overhauled
Oversaw
Planned
Presided
Prioritized
Produced
Recommended
Reorganized
Replaced
Restored
Reviewed
Scheduled
Secured
Selected
Streamlined
Strengthened
Supervised
Terminated

ORGANIZATIONAL SKILLS
Approved
Arranged
Catalogued
Categorized
Charted
Classified
Coded
Collected
Compiled
Corrected
Corresponded
Distributed
Executed
Filed
Generated
Incorporated
Inspected
Logged
Maintained
Monitored
Obtained
Operated
Ordered
Organized
Prepared
Processed
Provided
Purchased
Recorded
Registered
Reserved
Responded
Reviewed
Routed
Scheduled
Screened
Submitted

Action Verbs, *continued*

Supplied
Standardized
Systematized
Updated
Validated
Verified

RESEARCH SKILLS
Analyzed
Clarified
Collected
Compared
Conducted
Critiqued
Detected
Determined
Diagnosed
Evaluated
Examined
Experimented
Explored
Extracted
Formulated
Gathered
Inspected
Interviewed
Invented

Investigated
Located
Measured
Organized
Researched
Reviewed
Searched
Solved
Summarized
Surveyed
Systematized
Tested

TEACHING SKILLS
Adapted
Advised
Clarified
Coached
Communicated
Conducted
Coordinated
Critiqued
Developed
Enabled
Encouraged
Evaluated
Explained

Facilitated
Focused
Guided
Individualized
Informed
Instilled
Instructed
Motivated
Persuaded
Simulated
Stimulated
Taught
Tested
Trained
Transmitted
Tutored

TECHNICAL SKILLS
Adapted
Applied
Assembled
Built
Calculated
Computed
Conserved
Constructed
Converted

Debugged
Designed
Determined
Developed
Engineered
Fabricated
Fortified
Installed
Maintained
Operated
Overhauled
Printed
Programmed
Rectified
Regulated
Remodeled
Repaired
Replaced
Restored
Solved
Specialized
Standardized
Studied
Upgraded
Utilized

(Courtesy of Fairfax County, Virginia, website)

WORKSHEET 4.1 | *Choosing the Right Résumé Style*

	CHRONOLOGICAL RÉSUMÉ	SKILLS-BASED RÉSUMÉ
Related work experience	X	
Little or no related work experience		X
Related education	X	
Little related education		X
Poor work history with gaps		X
Frequent job changes		X
Work history shows career growth	X	
Impressive work history	X	
Out of workforce		X
Solid work history without gaps	X	

WORKSHEET 4.2 | *Chronological Résumé*

Heading (Including name, address, telephone number[s], and e-mail address):

Objective (Optional, but targeted toward specific job if used):

Summary/Qualifications (Hot buttons for your résumé "headline"):

Experience (Reverse chronological order, emphasizing accomplishments):

Education (Reverse chronological order):

WORKSHEET 4.3 \ *Skills-Based Résumé*

Heading (Including name, address, telephone number[s], and e-mail address):

Summary (Short overview of hot buttons):

Skills/Qualifications (Categorized by skill areas):

Experience (Basic information and brief overview):

Education (Reverse chronological order):

Sample Chronological Résumé

Jennifer Jobseeker
123 Main Street
Anywhere, VT 12345
(333) 333-3333
Jennifer.Jobseeker@xxx.com

QUALIFICATIONS

Experienced accountant with comprehensive skills in preparing, analyzing, and maintaining all types of accounting statements, records, and reports. Possess detailed knowledge of all government regulations and procedures. Effective problem solver able to investigate and resolve financial issues in a timely and thorough manner.

EXPERIENCE

Accounts R Us, Inc., Quaintville, Vermont (2002–Present)
Senior Staff Accountant

Support all company financial operations by performing complex accounting functions. Includes journal entries, income and balance sheet statements, account reconciliations, cost reports, and other accounting statements and reports.

- Conducted a study of accounting methods and procedures resulting in implementation of more efficient new procedures.
- Reviewed accuracy of journal entries, and developed a new process that reduced errors by 78%.
- Train all new junior accounting employees, relieving upper-level management of that responsibility.
- Created a document retention system for all legal and financial planning documents.

Jennifer Jobseeker, *page two*

Save-a-Buck Bookkeeping Services, Anywhere, Massachusetts (1997–2002)
Staff Accountant

Provided support to comptroller in all accounting-related functions.
Maintained all bookkeeping and accounting records, including bill paying
and monthly account reconciliation.

- Developed an innovative tickler system to ensure that cash flow
  obligations were tracked with 100% accuracy.
- Researched and recommended purchase of new financial tracking
  software.
- Discovered errors in bookkeeping system that saved the organization in
  excess of $25,000 annually.

EDUCATION

Anywhere Valley Community College, Anywhere, Massachusetts
A.A.S. in Accounting Systems

Sample Chronological Résumé (Electronic Version)

Jennifer Jobseeker
123 Main Street
Anywhere, VT 12345
(333) 333-3333
Jennifer.Jobseeker@xxx.com

Qualifications
Experienced accountant with comprehensive skills in preparing, analyzing, and maintaining all types of accounting statements, records, and reports. Possess detailed knowledge of all government regulations and procedures. Effective problem solver able to investigate and resolve financial issues in a timely and thorough manner.

Experience
Accounts R Us, Inc., Quaintville, Vermont (2002-Present)
Senior Staff Accountant
Support all company financial operations by performing complex accounting functions. Includes journal entries, income and balance sheet statements, account reconciliations, cost reports, and other accounting statements and reports.
* Conducted a study of accounting methods and procedures resulting in implementation of more efficient new procedures.
* Reviewed accuracy of journal entries, and developed a new process that reduced errors by 78%.
* Train all new junior accounting employees, relieving upper-level management of that responsibility.
*   Created a document retention system for all legal and financial planning documents.

Save-a-Buck Bookkeeping Services, Anywhere, Massachusetts (1997-2002)
Staff Accountant
Provided support to comptroller in all accounting-related functions. Maintained all bookkeeping and accounting records, including bill paying and monthly account reconciliation.
* Developed an innovative tickler system to ensure that cash flow obligations were tracked with 100% accuracy.

Jennifer Jobseeker, page two

* Researched and recommended purchase of new financial tracking software.
* Discovered errors in bookkeeping system that saved the organization in excess of $25,000 annually.

Education
Anywhere Valley Community College, Anywhere, Massachusetts
A.A.S. in Accounting Systems

Sample Skills-Based Résumé

Jason Jobseeker
123 Main Street
Anywhere, VT 12345
(333) 333-3333
Jason.Jobseeker@xxx.com

SUMMARY

Experienced human resources professional with background in compensation and benefits and labor relations and organizational development. Expertise in researching and implementing successful human resource information systems (HRIS).

QUALIFICATIONS

Compensation and Benefits
- Administered compensation system for company of more than 2,000 employees.
- Researched and contracted with new health benefits provider, resulting in a cost reduction of more than 35%.
- Developed and implemented new payroll system that eliminated ongoing errors in employee compensation.

Labor Relations
- Supervised labor relations function for a large industrial plan with more than 1,500 union employees.
- Led a negotiating team that averted a strike for the first time in more than ten years of contract negotiations.
- Partnered with union officials in promoting a safety initiative that reduced the plant accident rate by more than 50%.

Organizational Development
- Developed training for all line managers in coaching problem employees, leading to 20% drop in disciplinary actions.
- Designed and implemented matrix management system that allowed managers to supervise more efficient cross-functional teams.

Jason Jobseeker, *page two*

Human Resource Information Systems
- Researched and negotiated the purchase of a multi-million dollar HRIS.
- Implemented the system successfully, eliminating the need for hard copy record keeping.
- Saved more than $500,000 per year in administrative costs for paper copies of all documentation and records.

EXPERIENCE

Director, Human Resources
XYZ Industries, Smalltown, Vermont, 2002–Present
Supervise all functions of a comprehensive human resources function serving the needs of more than 2,500 local and 6,300 worldwide employees.

Human Resources Plant Manager
ZYX Association, Smallertown, Vermont, 1998–2002
Supervised the human resources function in a union facility of approximately 2,000 employees.

Compensation Specialist
Smallestown Central School District, Smallestown, Vermont, 1996–1998
Administered compensation for a public school district with about 350 employees.

EDUCATION

Great Education University, Bigtown, Vermont
M.B.A. with Human Resources concentration, 2004

Good Education University, Biggertown, Vermont
B.A. in Psychology, 1995

December 1, 2009

Jennifer Jobseeker
123 Main Street
Anywhere, VT 12345

Robert Robertson
Comptroller
XYZ Industries
145 South Street
Somewhere, VT 54321

Dear Mr. Robertson:

I noted with interested the advertisement on the XYZ Industries website for a Senior Accountant. After reviewing the job description for the position, I believe I have the ideal qualifications for the job. I'm writing to express my interest in meeting with you to discuss this position.

As you will see when you review my résumé, I possess extensive accounting experience. In my current position as a Senior Staff Accountant, I've implemented several programs to increase the effectiveness and efficiency of our accounting function. In particular, I researched and implemented several state-of-the-art changes to the accounting procedures we had been using. The end result was a much more efficient accounting operation with reduced errors.

My attached résumé includes more details about my successes and achievements in my current and previous position. I think you'll find that the skills and experience outlined make me an ideal candidate for your open position. I will follow up this correspondence with a phone call within the next week to set up an opportunity to meet with you about this opportunity. Thank you for your consideration.

Sincerely,

Jennifer Jobseeker

Enclosure

Sample Skills-Based Cover Letter

December 1, 2010

Jennifer Jobseeker
123 Main Street
Anywhere, VT 12345

Robert Robertson
Comptroller
XYZ Industries
145 South Street
Somewhere, VT 54321

Dear Mr. Robertson:

I noted with interested the advertisement on the XYZ Industries website for a Senior Accountant. After reviewing the job description for the position, I believe that I have the ideal qualifications for the job. Based on the major skill sets in your job description, here are my qualifications:

Your Requirements
- Handle Complex Accounting Functions
- Knowledge of Accounting Software
- Detail Orientation
- Improving Efficiency

My Qualifications
- As a senior staff accountant, currently perform all complex accounting functions
- Researched accounting software and made recommendations for purchase
- Developed and implemented new document retention system
- Developed new journal entry process that reduced errors by 78%

My attached résumé further details the qualifications outlined above and provides more information about my successes and achievements in my current and previous positions. I will follow up this correspondence with a phone call within the next week to set up an opportunity to meet with you about this opportunity. Thank you for your consideration.

Sincerely,

Jennifer Jobseeker

Enclosure

PART 2

The Multi-Channel Approach

The number one mistake made by most job hunters is relying on just one or two primary channels or strategies to pursue their job searches. They find something they are comfortable with and do little else. Much of your competition will take a single-channel approach, so simply by using a variety of strategies you gain an edge in a tough job market.

Most commonly, I find clients relying on the Internet as their only job search strategy. Whether they respond to Internet job ads or post on Internet job boards, many job seekers feel that this is the only way to look for a job in the twenty-first century. This is also a comfortable strategy for many people because it can be accomplished primarily from home and doesn't require a lot of personal contact or rejection. This is the single biggest mistake that I see people make in pursuing their job search.

Chapter 5 is devoted exclusively to networking. Many people are resistant to this practice, but the statistics consistently show that the majority of job seekers find their next job through either personal or professional networks. The advent of electronic networking has only increased the importance of this job-hunting strategy. Done properly, networking can benefit all parties involved and be an integral part of your approach.

Relying on just one or two strategies will definitely extend the length of your search and hinder your success. You will need to get out of your comfort zone and try some techniques that are new and different. You may resist the methods you aren't familiar with, but a wide range of approaches will speed your search and get you to your goal sooner. In a tough job market, the most crucial wisdom is to use a variety of strategies and leave no stone unturned.

The chapters in this part examine the range of typical job search techniques, including networking, online strategies, job fairs, and a host of other ideas. We'll take a look at some strategies that are less common and more innovative than those your competitors may be using. A variety of worksheets and exercises will ensure that you make the most of each technique described.

Networking 2.0

Where to Find New and Better Networks

In a tough job search environment, building effective networks *must* be an important part of your job search strategy. Because employers are fearful of being buried in an avalanche of electronic résumés, many positions are never even advertised externally. That means that you must have "inside" contacts who know what is really going on in your field and where the potential opportunities are. Building and maintaining strong professional networks is the best way to develop those inside contacts.

Many job seekers avoid building networks like the plague. They're not comfortable with meeting strangers or remote acquaintances, and the idea of having to get "out there" and deal with people in person scares them. One common defense I hear is "I don't like using people." But if you do it properly, building and maintaining a network isn't "using" people. Instead, it is about taking the time and effort to build healthy relationships that you and those in your networks benefit from.

In this chapter we'll examine building both traditional in-person networks as well as virtual online networks. Nothing beats strong personal networks of people you see and interact with regularly, of course. But in an era when many people are more mobile in their job searches, an online network can be extremely valuable, particularly in helping you develop opportunities outside of your immediate geographic area.

WHY SHOULD YOU BUILD NETWORKS?

The bottom line in any discussion of networking is that most people find their next job through networking. Whether through friends, colleagues, or family, the vast majority of jobs are found through the strength of personal and professional networks. The numbers vary depending on which survey you consult, but overall the statistics show this to be true more than 70 percent of the time.

We'll look at a range of networking techniques in this chapter and examine the strengths of interpersonal networking and some of the newer online networking options. You'll gain a much better understanding of the benefits of networking. We'll also examine some common networking scenarios and how to handle them. You'll understand why you should *always* be actively networking, even when you are not involved in a job search.

Let's see how Mary's attempts at networking go.

MARY TRIES TO BUILD A NETWORK

As Mary's job search dragged on, she knew that she needed to try some new strategies. In one magazine article, she read about the benefits of networking in a job search. *Hmmm,* she thought, *this article says that more than half of job seekers find their next job through networking. I tried to network at that reception I went to a few weeks ago, but it sure didn't work very well. Maybe I should give it another try.*

Mary decided that she would start by calling several of her former coworkers. Some had found new jobs, so maybe they would know about opportunities. She decided to start with Barbara. She had worked with Barbara for more than five years. Although they had never been close, they had eaten lunch together several times. After several tries, Mary got Barbara on the phone.

"Hi, Barbara," said Mary brightly. "I hear that you started a new job at XYZ Corporation." "That's right," answered Barbara. "I've been here for about three weeks and I really love it so far. It's a really good place to work." *Ah,* thought Mary, *this sounds promising.* "I really need to find a job soon," said Mary. "Could you please take my résumé to Human Resources at XYZ and tell them that you know me and I'm great? I would really appreciate it!"

Because Barbara had never been close to Mary, this request caught her a little off guard. She would have been more than happy to talk with Mary about the company and what their challenges seemed to be, but this overt request, out of the blue, was pretty assertive.

After a few moments of uncomfortable silence, Barbara said, "Well, send me your résumé, and I'll see what I can do. You have to remember that I am still very new here." *Sounds like she's trying to get out of this,* thought Mary. *You would think she would want to help me.* "Okay, I'll e-mail it to you," said Mary and hung up the phone. *I just don't understand how this networking business works,* thought Mary. *Isn't the purpose to help me?*

WHAT SHOULD YOU DO IF YOU'RE STILL EMPLOYED?

The best time to build a network is while you are still employed. That is, of course, easier said than done! Many of us are working long hours and have a wide range of personal commitments outside the workplace. Finding the time to build and maintain a professional network is difficult. You must, however, build the time into your schedule to do so. Not only will a strong network help when you are searching for a job, but it can help you in your professional life generally. Wouldn't it be nice to be able to pick up the phone and call a colleague for advice on that tough project you are trying to complete? A strong network will benefit you now and later!

The easiest way to start your network is with current and past colleagues. Our coworkers tend to pass in and out of our lives. Nowadays, we stay in positions for a shorter time on average than in the past. Despite good intentions and promises made during a coworker's going away party, we often drift away from each other. Simply staying in touch a few times a year, either by e-mail or in person, will keep you on each other's radar screens. It's not a whole lot of effort and can really pay off when you need professional advice or when you do find yourself looking for a new job.

Professional associations also offer a myriad of networking opportunities. But simply joining and going to a few meetings isn't enough. You need to get involved in some way. One of my clients recently told me that at the local chapter of his professional association he has been the volunteer who greets and hosts new members when they come to their first meeting. Other members considered it kind of a thankless job, so everyone was delighted when he volunteered to take it on. My client says that he now has a huge network just from this simple activity he has performed for the past four years. The new members are always grateful for his friendly face at that first meeting and continue to seek him out when they see him at meetings. Several are now colleagues whom he frequently sees for a cup of coffee or lunch.

Volunteer opportunities within your company can be a great way to build an internal network. They offer the chance to meet friends and colleagues outside of your immediate group or department whom you might not otherwise interact with. This can elevate your reputation within the organization as you become more widely known. It can also give you the inside track when internal opportunities arise. This internal network can become an external network over time, as people come and go.

Most organizations have a variety of volunteer opportunities. These opportunities take time and effort in addition to the stress of the full-time job you are already working. But in the long run, taking advantage of volunteer opportunities can really pay off—and you might even enjoy yourself. An employee at one large corporation volunteered to serve on the committee for the annual United Way campaign. Eventually, she became the chair of the committee and developed a broad network while gaining valuable leadership experience that served her well and made her proud.

Regardless of how you do it, make a commitment to yourself to begin to build a professional network, especially if you are currently employed. The benefits will be both immediate and long range.

WHAT IF YOU'RE NO LONGER EMPLOYED?

Even if you're no longer employed, it's critical that you build your network. The following exercise is very easy and will help you build a comprehensive prioritized network.

The Refrigerator Exercise

It is never too late to begin to build a network. Even if you didn't build a strong professional network while you were employed, it should be one of your first priorities after becoming unemployed. The first step in the process is to determine exactly the people you should approach. One way of doing this is through the "refrigerator exercise." Research says the average person goes to the refrigerator approximately twenty-seven times a day. What better place to build your networking list? Use the "refrigerator exercise" in Worksheet 5.1 at the end of this chapter. The worksheet breaks down the various people in your life into categories that will help you identify more of them. Follow this process:

1. Post the worksheet on the front of your refrigerator. Leave it there for at least one week. Add more sheets if you run out of space.
2. Each time you go to your refrigerator, try to record the name of at least one person you know. Do not be concerned at this point about whether that person does the same type of work you do or whether you think he or she might be helpful in your search. Simply record the name. Include the person's employer and the type of work the person does if you know it.
3. After recording names for at least one week, take down your completed sheets.
4. Add any missing employer and job information.
5. Finally, prioritize everyone on your list according to how knowledgeable you think they are about your career field and how helpful you think they can be in your networking efforts. Label people who work in your field or whom you know well with an "A." Label people who work in other fields or whom you know less well on your worksheet as "B." Casual acquaintances should be labeled "C."

This exercise will result in the basis for your networking list.

How Do You Start to Build Your Network?

You'll probably want to start building your network with your "A" list from your refrigerator exercise. These people fall into two categories:

○ You know them well, and they will be open to helping you.
○ They work in your field and may have valuable professional information and contacts.

Now is the time to make sure you will not be construed as "using" people. In Mary's scenario, she reconnected with someone she had not spoken to in a while and moved immediately to ask for help. The contact was unprepared and unhappy with Mary's approach and, as a result, will probably do little or nothing to benefit Mary's cause. Mary was a "networking user," which won't get her far.

Instead, think about what you can bring to the table that might be of benefit to your potential networking contacts. Maybe you read an article about a recent advancement in your field that you think would be of interest. In some cases, you may know that a contact has a professional need or problem that you might be able to help him or her with. Perhaps you have a unique expertise that you would be willing to share. Whatever the case, think long and hard about what you can offer to the networking relationship. It should really be a two-way street, and your contacts will be much more willing to help you if you are offering something in return.

If a networking contact is able to help you in some way, show the common courtesies that we were taught when young. Write a thank-you note, give a small gift, or buy lunch or a cup of coffee. The contact may not be able to do anything to help you right now, but you want the relationship to continue. Show your gratitude appropriately, and make sure the person knows that you will be available should he or she need assistance in the future. This two-way street is the true aim of networking.

HOW DO YOU MANAGE YOUR NETWORK?

Your network may end up having so many people in it that you'll find it difficult to manage. The tips that follow will help you manage all your contacts effectively.

How Should You Contact Your Network Prospects?

There is no "best" way to contact the prospects on your networking list. How you contact each person will depend on his or her availability and the circumstances. For example, is the person local or located some distance away? How well do you already know the person?

E-mail is probably the least desirable method of contact. Most people are inundated with e-mail messages every day. Yours could easily be overlooked or deleted, especially if it's not identified as being of high priority.

Either phone or in-person contact will work best in most situations. The immediacy and perceived urgency of a phone call is more likely to elicit a response than an e-mail message. Both phone and in-person contacts offer a better opportunity to build rapport with your contact. Networking is all about building relationships, so the personal rapport is critical.

How Do You Maintain Your Network?

A network should not be a series of one-time contacts but a series of ongoing relationships. A networking contact that isn't able to help you today may be able to help you next month and vice versa. It's imperative that you have an organized plan for staying in regular contact with the people in your network. Many job hunters find it helpful to put together a chart or spreadsheet to record their contacts. A template for keeping records about your networking contacts is shown in Worksheet 5.2.

Keep notes about each of your networking contacts and your interactions with them. It's particularly useful to keep information about what issues and challenges they face. As you read articles and conduct research about your career field, you may find a piece of information that may be helpful to one or more of your contacts. What a great reason to get in contact with them again! The best part is that you're not making contact because you need something from them but because you have something to provide them. Your networking relationship becomes a true two-way, back-and-forth relationship.

What Is an Interview for Information?

You may be able to arrange an opportunity for an informational interview through one of your networking contacts. An informational interview is a chance to have a conversation with someone who can provide you with more information about your career field or information about a specific employer or industry in which you may have an interest. An informational interview is *not* a job interview and should not be treated as such.

To prepare for an informational interview, think about what kinds of information/data would be helpful to know about a particular field, industry, or company. Prepare a list of questions and be ready to play the "interviewer" in this situation because you will be questioning your contact for information. Going into the meeting without at least a partial list of questions will result in an awkward or unhelpful conversation. One recent college graduate scored an informational interview with a prominent figure in his chosen field. He carefully dressed in his best suit for the appointment but prepared no questions. When he arrived and sat down across from the executive, the executive simply looked at him and asked, "What can I do for you?" With no questions prepared, the recent grad squandered this rare opportunity.

During the informational interview, be sensitive to any time constraints your contact may have. If time parameters weren't established when you arranged the meeting, ask at the beginning how much time will be available, and show the courtesy of not exceeding those constraints.

Do take a copy of your résumé along to the meeting, but offer it *only* if requested. Some contacts will want a copy of your résumé to have on hand in case a suitable opportunity should arise, but the explicit purpose of the meeting is only to get more information that will be valuable to your search. Trying to turn this opportunity into a job interview might offend your contact, if he or she feels you've arranged the meeting under false pretenses.

If you make a good impression, however, future opportunities could result. Several years ago at the request of a colleague, I did an informational interview with a young woman just out of graduate school. She was professional and articulate and had prepared some excellent questions. I was impressed and remembered her. A little more than a month later, I had an unexpected opening on my staff. Whom do you think I called and encouraged to apply? I ended up hiring her as a direct result of that impressive informational interview.

Be sure to send a thank-you note or e-mail to follow up on your informational interview. Not only is this a polite gesture that will make a good impression, but it also will remind your contact one more time of the positive impression you made.

HOW SHOULD YOU HANDLE COMMON NETWORKING SCENARIOS?

Networking can happen in all kinds of ways, at both small professional meetings and large professional conferences. Both can be intimidating if you're not prepared.

Attend a Local Professional Association Meeting

One of the most common networking scenarios is attending a meeting of a local professional organization. You will meet people from the area who work in your career field and also learn more about what is going on in your field. The advantages to you are that the event will likely be small and manageable in size and you'll gain exposure in your local geographic area.

You should have a networking goal in mind when you attend a local association meeting. That goal should *not* be to find a job. Your goal might be to just strike up one or two solid professional acquaintances with whom you can develop a professional relationship. Or, your goal might be to find out more about what is happening in a particular part of your career field. Whatever your goal, having one will help you strike up and hold meaningful conversations.

Attend a Major Professional Conference

Major (national) conferences are among the scariest of networking scenarios. Hundreds or even thousands of people are milling around, attending sessions and mingling at receptions—it can feel like you are the only person who doesn't know anyone. How can you possibly meet anyone or begin any kind of conversation?

First, be sure to take advantage of any opportunities built into the program. One major conference that I attend sponsors what it calls "Meet to Eat" each evening during the conference. It's a service you can sign up for that matches you with a group of people to meet and have dinner with nearby. Because the groups are small, it's not intimidating, and the other people who register are also on their own and looking to meet and interact with other conference attendees. It's been a great opportunity for me to meet professional colleagues in a nonthreatening setting, and I've developed ongoing relationships with several.

When attending a conference session, arrive a few minutes early and look for someone sitting alone. As you wait for the presentation to begin, it's relatively easy to strike up a conversation about the content of the upcoming session. You may find that you and the other person share a strong interest in the topic— after all, you're both there!

The worst nightmare for most conference participants is the dreaded reception. Everyone seems to know everyone else, sipping drinks in groups and having a great time. Once again, look for someone standing or sitting alone. He or she is likely in the same situation as you are. Politely approach that person, introduce yourself, and strike up a conversation about the conference and what he or she has gleaned from it so far. That person will probably be grateful that you stopped to talk. And remember, most of the people talking and laughing have just met each other, too!

Notice that none of these approaches centers on job hunting. They focus on meeting new colleagues and generating new professional relationships. Jumping into job search mode without first carefully building a relationship will only scare people away. Once they know you—even just a little bit—they're much more likely to help you.

HOW DO YOU DEVELOP AND MAINTAIN YOUR ELECTRONIC NETWORK?

The most recent development in networking has been the advent of online networking tools. Whether designed for business networking or social networking, these tools almost immediately became valuable tools for the job hunter. Online networks can also work against you, however, so you really must understand how they work and how to use them before you start. From the profile you create to how you approach potential contacts, these networks require just as much finesse as in-person networking.

Creating Your Profile

Write your profile with great care when registering for any networking site. Put the same time and thought into your profile that you put into developing your résumé. Just as your résumé is usually the first impression an employer has of you, your profile will be the first impression that any online contact has of you. A carelessly written profile or one that has potentially harmful personal information can turn a potential contact completely off. In addition to your content, pay attention to your writing tone, spelling, and grammar.

Joining Groups of Like-Minded Individuals

Some online networking sites, like LinkedIn and Facebook, allow you to form or join groups of people with whom you have something in common. Groups exist for people who work in the same career fields, share common professional interests, or are alumni of the same school. Any group you share a commonality with gives you an automatic starting place for discussions with the other members.

You must show respect in your interactions with the other members of any group you join. Immediately soliciting help with your job search will only turn members of the group off, especially since you are merely another username at this point. Instead, read posts carefully, looking for areas where you can provide advice and input. Begin to build relationships based on common interests, and offer to help others with their challenges and problems. Building these connections will help you develop a group of allies who are willing to reach out and assist you.

Connecting with Contacts of Your Network Members

One of the advantages of online networking is that you can view the members of your contacts' networks. You will often find that your contacts are connected to people who could be potentially helpful to you. But how do you reach out to members of your contacts' networks?

The most important step is to ask your contacts before attempting to reach their contacts. In addition to being the courteous thing to do, it ensures that your contact can give you some insight into the person you are contacting and how to best approach him or her. Better yet, your contact may be willing to facilitate the connection. Your contact will also have a chance to warn you away from someone who doesn't want to be contacted, saving you time and effort. In any case, be sure to treat the members of your contacts' networks with the same respect you use with your own contacts.

Contacting People with Whom You Don't Have a Connection

Another advantage of online networking is the ability to search for people you don't know by job title, company name, and so on. You can probably find total strangers with whom you share common interests, who work in your career field, or who work for organizations that are of interest to you.

Again, how you approach these people is critical. Many will indicate in their profiles whether they are open to unsolicited networking. Some make it clear that they are not. If they're not, don't push the issue by contacting them. Nothing good will come of reaching out to people who don't want to be contacted.

If you do find a stranger open to contact, use the same approach and courtesies that you would use in person. Based on the person's profile, are there areas of expertise you have that might allow you to help with his or her likely challenges? Can you find a commonality that will help ease the initial contact? Make sure that the initial contact is friendly but not too familiar. Give yourself an opportunity to build a rapport before asking for the information or assistance that you think the person might be able to offer.

Managing Your Online Presence

In an era when employers frequently check networking sites and do online searches to see what they can find about candidates, being aware of your online presence is critical. You may be aware of what you have posted on various networking sites and what is on your personal website, but you may not know everything that others have posted about you online. Something you don't even know about could be lurking out there and could damage your job-hunting prospects.

I strongly suggest that you regularly conduct an online search for yourself. When I did it, I was surprised to find that friends I had vacationed with had posted on their website captioned pictures of our trip. Because the pictures were captioned by name, their site showed up when I did a search for myself. There was nothing horribly damaging (other than a picture of me in a swimming pool with my beverage of choice), but I didn't want those pictures to be part of the results when someone did a search for me. I asked to have the pictures removed and my friends willingly did so. I now do a search for myself every few months to see what is out there.

Observing Online Etiquette

The way you conduct yourself online will have a direct impact on how successful you are at building online professional relationships. Being too aggressive will turn people off (or even offend them) and make them reluctant to interact with you, yet you must also be assertive enough to make your presence known. It's a tough balancing act, but here are some hints about appropriate etiquette:

○ Although you see only a computer screen, remember that you are communicating with a person on the other end. Whether you are corresponding by e-mail or posting comments in a discussion group, someone is reading your comments on the other end. Carefully consider both the tone and content of what you're writing and whether it could be misinterpreted. The classic, and still best, test is to ask yourself, *Would I actually say this in person?*
○ Remember that anything you write could come back to haunt you. It is unnervingly simple for anyone to save something that you have written, and if it is objectionable or offensive

it could be shared with countless others or show up again at some point in the future.

○ Learn about the "culture" of an online domain before you post. One colleague suggests "lurking before leaping." Monitor the ongoing conversations and chats for a bit. Get a feel for the tone and what is acceptable in a particular domain. Don't actively participate until after you feel certain that you can conform to the norms.

○ Consider your online image. Because you are attempting to build professional online relationships, you need to project a professional image. Many of us have a tendency to get careless (especially in an online chat environment), forgetting the basic rules of spelling and grammar. Your writing is all that people can judge you by in this environment, so how you present yourself is important. Also be sure that you actually know what you are writing about and stick to topics in which you have expertise. A fraud will stick out in an online environment.

○ Here too, don't be just a "taker." Offer up your knowledge and resources to the people who you meet virtually. By exchanging your expertise with others, you can build up a reservoir of goodwill. Your online colleagues will be much more willing to provide assistance to you if it's a two-way relationship.

KEVIN'S NETWORKS

Kevin had read several articles that had convinced him of the importance of networking as one of his job search strategies. He knew the statistics show the majority of job hunters find their next position through networking contacts. He had developed a comprehensive list of potential networking contacts and prioritized those contacts. But what should he do next to initiate communication with some of his contacts?

One of Kevin's "A" priority contacts was his new neighbor John, whom he had met at the recent community association meeting. He knew from their conversation that John worked in his career field and might be in a position to know about job opportunities. What would be the best way to get in contact with John?

Kevin decided to pick up the phone and make a call. Although he did have John's e-mail address, Kevin knew that the immediacy of a phone call would give him a better chance of a real conversation. He picked up the phone and dialed John's number. John was at his desk and picked up the phone on the second ring.

"Hi, John, this is Kevin."

"Kevin," said John. "It's good to hear from you. How are you?"

"I'm fine," answered Kevin. "Just trying to get in contact again with some folks I haven't talked with in a while. How are things with you?"

"They're pretty good," answered John. "Just an awful lot going on, as usual! Are you familiar with the impact of the Smith Act on our business?"

"Oh, yes," said Kevin. "I was dealing with that a lot in recent months. It was a real challenge. In fact, I have some ideas that might be helpful in your situation. Would you like to grab a cup of coffee in the next few days and talk?"

"Oh, thanks," answered John. "That would be great! I can use all the advice I can get. If you've had some experience with this, you know what a mess it is."

"I should also tell you," said Kevin, "that I got caught up in the last layoff at my company. If you have any thoughts or advice when we get together, that would be great!"

"Oh, I heard about that downsizing," said John. "I'll think about some contacts and what I know before we get together. I'm really glad that you called and look forward to getting together."

WORKSHEET 5.1 | *Refrigerator Exercise*

	NAME	EMPLOYER	TYPE OF WORK	PRIORITY: A, B, C
Colleagues				
Friends				

WORKSHEET 5.1

	NAME	EMPLOYER	TYPE OF WORK	PRIORITY: A, B, C
Family				
Neighbors				

WORKSHEET 5.1 CONTINUED

	NAME	EMPLOYER	TYPE OF WORK	PRIORITY: A, B, C
Community Contacts				
Other				

WORKSHEET 5.2   *Networking Contacts Log*

NAME	CONTACT DATE	METHOD OF CONTACT (PHONE, E-MAIL, IN PERSON)	DISCUSSION	FOLLOW-UP

Résumé Websites

Why They Usually Don't Work, and How to Make Them Work for You

The ease of access and wide range of resources on the Internet has changed the way millions of people conduct their job searches. Gone are the days of spending money on postage to mail cover letters and résumés. Gone are the endless hours spent in the library conducting research about potential employers. *Almost* gone are the days of scouring newspaper advertisements looking for appropriate job opportunities.

With the convenience, however, come some pitfalls. In this chapter we'll examine why Internet listings don't always work well for the job hunter, and what you'll need to do—especially in a tough market—to stand out on the Internet.

THE INTERNET: BLESSING AND CURSE

Because the Internet has fundamentally changed the way that most of us look for a job, it's been both a blessing and a curse for many job hunters. Of course, the ease of use and instant access to vast amounts of information are invaluable. But it can also be a killer because of its addictive power and the ubiquity that makes otherwise conscientious job hunters ignore other important techniques that may prove just as productive. Much has been written recently about online addiction in general, and it can be a critical issue in a job search.

But the Web's biggest flaw is that in a tough economy, way too many job hunters depend solely on it as their preferred job search tool. They post their résumés on all the major job boards, troll for online job postings every day, and do countless Internet searches for opportunities. These are certainly all strategies that any job hunter should use, but most make two mistakes that you must avoid:

○ They use only basic Internet search strategies.
○ They don't strategize more innovative ways to use the Internet in their search.

You will outwit your competition if you avoid these two mistakes. In fact, some career counselors recommend that you limit online time to only 25 percent of the total time you dedicate to your job search. To make the best use of the time you spend online, make sure that you have specific goals for what you want to accomplish. You'll waste much less time!

───────────────○───────────────

MARY'S INTERNET JOB SEARCH

Mary had been an avid Internet user ever since its early days. She loved Internet shopping and treasured the convenience that the Internet offered her busy life. As she thought about how to conduct her job search, she just knew that the Internet would be a fantastic resource.

Sitting down at her computer, Mary reflected on what she had read about Internet job search resources. *The first thing I should do,* she thought, *is to get my résumé posted on all those big job search boards. I read that employers search those boards all the time looking for well-qualified candidates like me.* She quickly identified several major job search sites, registered, and posted her résumé.

Mary also knew that she should set up some search agents on several of the sites where she had posted her résumé. Search agents would look for opportunities according to parameters that she set, and any appropriate job opportunities would automatically be sent to her e-mail inbox. *This is great,* she thought. *I don't even have to go through the job listings and search. Anything that is suitable will automatically be sent to me. Boy, the Internet sure makes job searching easy!* With that, Mary logged off her computer, confident that she had done all she could to take advantage of Internet job search resources.

A couple of days later, Mary's phone rang.

"Hello," said the voice at the other end. "This is Wally Williams from Insurance Land, Inc. I found your résumé on one of the big job boards, and I'm really impressed with your background. How would you like to come in for an interview for a management position with us?"

Mary was thrilled to have a response so quickly and eagerly made an appointment with Wally for an interview early the following week.

On the day of the interview, Mary arrived about ten minutes early. She took several deep breaths and composed herself as she waited for her interview. At the appointed time Wally appeared and introduced himself, smiling broadly.

"Hi, Mary," he said. "Come on in and let's talk about the great opportunity I have for you."

This is great, thought Mary. *I really need this opportunity!* Wally spoke enthusiastically about his company while asking Mary questions about her background. She noticed, however, that he said little about the actual job or its responsibilities.

When it appeared that the interview was nearing an end, she felt compelled to ask about the details of exactly what the job would entail. As she listened to Wally enthusiastically describe the opportunity, she quickly realized that it was a commission-only sales job. There would be no regular salary, nor any guarantee of what she would make on commission. Wally spoke enthusiastically about one "superstar" salesman and how much he earned each year but didn't mention anyone else. Mary's heart fell. This was not the "management" job that she had anticipated hearing about. She wasn't interested in sales, and certainly not in a job that offered no regular guaranteed salary. *This guy is obviously searching the boards looking for any and all prospects,* she thought, *and I fell for it.*

In the weeks that followed, Mary got several other "hits" from the résumés she had posted on various job boards. What they all had in common was that very little information was offered up front, simply the offer of an in-person interview. *I really thought that I would get more hits for "real" jobs,* thought Mary, as she perused the job boards over yet another morning cup of coffee, looking for appropriate opportunities.

BASICS OF USING MAJOR JOB SEARCH BOARDS

You should certainly take advantage of all that the major job search boards have to offer. They can be an effective resource if used properly. You should use the basic utilities like posting your résumé and setting up search agents. You will certainly get hits you're not interested in and probably be contacted about business deals that you would rather pass on, but you never know what employer might see your résumé or what job might be posted that is perfect.

It is very important to make sure your posted résumé is of the highest quality and contains the skills most commonly required in your career field. Much of your competition, eager to get something posted as quickly as possible, will post a poor résumé without thinking about important skill sets. It may not do a good job of marketing the individual (remember avoiding the résumé as autobiography?), or it may be filled with spelling and grammatical errors. To stand out, your posted résumé must highlight the most critical skills and be grammatically perfect. You obviously can't customize your résumé the way you would if applying for a specific opportunity, but you can make sure that it is letter-perfect and includes the skills you know are important in your field.

Another good idea is to set up search agents with different sets of keywords related to both your technical and transferable skill sets. Many job descriptions and advertisements are written by managers who don't know how to write a good description. They know what they need and want but don't know how to articulate it in a written ad. Other ads are written by human resources representatives who *don't* totally understand the job or the necessary skills. In either case, having multiple search agents set up with different sets of keywords will help to ensure that nothing that could be appropriate slips by. Also, most job boards use automated tools to scan the résumés of applicants. If the tool doesn't find the keywords (skills) in your résumé, you will automatically be eliminated from consideration.

GOING ABOVE AND BEYOND IN USING THE MAJOR JOB SEARCH BOARDS

Suppose you do get a hit with one of your search agents, and a job shows up in your e-mail inbox that is perfect for you. The problem is that hundreds of other people are probably perfect for the job as well. Yes, having a great résumé will help, but how else do you stand out against what will probably be very tough competition? After all, this job was posted on a major job board viewed by millions of people every day! How can you get ahead of the competition?

Inside Connections—Personal

This will take extra effort, but you've got to find a way to get a connection inside the organization. If the company is local, does anyone in your network know anyone inside the company? You may be lucky enough to find someone inside the company who has some knowledge of the available position or who knows the hiring manager. Even if your contact doesn't have direct knowledge about the job, the person may be willing to scout around and see what he or she can find out. Since many organizations pay bonuses to employees who make successful referrals, your internal contacts may be particularly eager to help because they'll get something out of it too.

Inside Connections—Electronic

If the company isn't local (or if it is and you can't locate a personal contact), can you find a connection through any of your online groups or networks (on LinkedIn, Facebook, etc.)? There are risks involved in trying to develop a connection through your online network, but it may be worth it depending on how perfect the job is for you. Remember, a second- or third-level contact may not be as interested in helping you. Just as with your other networking opportunities, you should look for a way to give back. Read his or her online profile and look for areas of common interest or possible challenges. If you can find a commonality or give input about a possible challenge, your chances of a favorable response to a request for assistance are much better.

Whatever route you take, your chances of landing the job greatly improve if you can find an inside contact within an organization. Even if your contact is only able to give you more insight into organizational culture, every piece of knowledge helps you figure out what it will take to get hired. Organizations do pay attention to the recommendations of their employees, and many hiring decisions are influenced by current employees. Going above and beyond can make that job opening you see on one of the major job boards a reality!

Newspaper Websites

Remember when leafing through the newspaper want ads used to be the preferred method for finding a new job? Most newspapers now have an online presence in addition to their print editions. This online presence usually includes some kind of electronic classified listings. Although the newspapers may still publish help wanted ads in their print editions, the new job opportunities will typically hit their online job boards much earlier.

Most of the major big city newspapers, such at the *Washington Post*, maintain their own classified listings. They can be a good resource for locating opportunities within the geographic region served by the newspaper. In some cases they even conduct periodic online "job fairs." Newspapers in smaller cities have found it expensive and difficult to maintain their own independent listings. Their websites will typically link to whatever major job board they have contracted with and allow you to do a local search on that job board. That's not much different from visiting the major job board on your own, so not particularly valuable.

But either way, part of your online strategy should be to visit the newspaper websites for any geographic areas in which you are interested. You may find information about jobs that have only been advertised locally. If you do find a "hit," follow the same strategies outlined previously for opportunities found on a major job board. In addition to applying for the job, search for some kind of inside connection, either personal or electronic.

Targeted Websites

Many websites now provide information and services (including job listings) for particular designated groups of people. These groups can include people of various ethnic groups, age groups, or other special populations. Employers who list jobs on these sites often have a particular interest in servicing the populations targeted by the sites.

For example, Saludos Web (saludos.com) serves people of Hispanic descent. Workforce50.com (workforce50.com) serves the age 50+ workforce. If you are part of a group served by a targeted website, the site can be a valuable resource in your job search.

PROFESSIONAL ASSOCIATION JOB BOARDS

We discussed professional associations as a resource in Chapter 5. You probably remember that they can be valuable as a networking resource and that you can find professional associations in your field through the American Society of Association Executives website (asaecenter.org).

Most professional associations also maintain job boards on their national or international websites, which are typically open to the general public. Many employers (especially in tough economic times) prefer to post their jobs on the boards run by professional associations, rather than the huge job sites. They find that it is more efficient to promote the opening to a targeted audience of likely candidates rather than posting on one of the major job boards. This makes these boards an invaluable resource, as the caliber of jobs tends to be higher and each posting will not necessarily result in a deluge of résumés.

After looking at the job boards on national and international association websites, search for websites of local chapters of the national associations you've identified. Many local chapters also maintain local job boards specific to the career field, and you'll find job listings limited to the geographic area covered by the chapter. Some employers prefer to use the local job boards rather than the national association boards because they're only interested in local candidates. The competition will be much less intense than if the job had appeared on a national or international job board.

One additional hint about professional association job boards . . . these boards are typically coordinated by an association member who volunteers for the responsibility. That person's contact information is often displayed on the website. These folks are particularly rich resources because they really have their fingers on the pulse of the job market in your field. They've most likely volunteered for the responsibility because they are interested in helping others in their profession. My experience has been that they are generally very willing to share their knowledge about the job market, and are often able to provide some great job search ideas specific to your career field and the market in their area.

Company Websites

Earlier in this book, you went through an exercise that helped you narrow your search down to the level of individual companies. Check the websites of those on your target list for their job boards. In a time of economic recession, many companies elect to post their job openings *only* on their websites, so as to limit the flood of résumés. This means you must regularly check the websites of any companies you are interested in. Many will allow you to set up a search agent, just as the major job boards do, so that any jobs fitting your parameters will automatically be e-mailed to you.

The additional benefit of perusing company websites is that you may be able to locate contact information for someone in the organization's human resources office. If approached carefully and with respect, that person may be able to help if you get bogged down in the electronic application process.

U.S. Government

Interested in working for Uncle Sam? Even in tough economic times, jobs with the federal government are generally plentiful and varied, both in career field and geographic location. Be forewarned, however, that the application and interview process can be lengthy and tedious. The Office of Personnel Management (OPM) has made some progress in recent years in simplifying the process and shortening the time required, but it's still more complex and time-consuming than the private sector. For those who make it through, many federal opportunities offer interesting and challenging work, pay quite well, and include great benefits.

To make it easier to investigate federal opportunities, a centralized federal government job website is available at usajobs .gov. On a recent visit, more than 37,000 U.S. government job opportunities were posted. With a large portion of the federal workforce eligible for retirement over the next few years, that number isn't likely to go down. You can search in a variety of ways, including zip code and keyword(s). You'll probably be surprised at how many federal opportunities are spread throughout the United States (and sometimes internationally). The options are not restricted to the Washington, D.C., area. It's definitely worth a visit to see what opportunities might be available.

If you apply for a federal job, be very careful about following the application procedures to the letter. You will need to complete a federal-style résumé—you can find samples of these online—including all the information specifically requested in the ad. Be sure that your résumé addresses every skill mentioned in the job announcement. Many federal agencies use an automated tool called Resumix to scan the résumés of applicants. If the tool doesn't find the keywords (skills) in your résumé, you will automatically be eliminated from consideration.

In addition, you will probably be asked to write answers to several questions about your knowledge, skills, and abilities (commonly called KSAs). Answer these questions completely and with very specific examples. If your answers are incomplete (particularly if they don't have specific examples of how you've used or displayed the KSA), you will be automatically eliminated.

Many applicants for federal jobs (both internally for transfers and from the outside) struggle mightily with writing effective responses to the KSAs. Here's a possible format that may ease the pain of answering them. Consider these three factors in order:

○ **Situation:** What was the specific situation that you encountered when you used or displayed the skill? Provide enough concise detail so that the reader can understand the basics of the situation and why the skill was important.

○ **Actions:** What were some of the actions that you took in addressing the situation? Again, be very specific about the actions. Zero in on what you specifically did even if it was part of a group response.

○ **Results:** What were the outcomes/results? How did your skills relate to the success that you achieved?

───────────────○───────────────

KEVIN'S INTERNET JOB SEARCH

Kevin had been perusing the various job boards on the Internet for the past several days. He had posted his résumé on the major job boards, set up search agents, and responded to a few jobs he had seen advertised that appeared to be a good fit. One morning, Kevin suddenly found a job that looked perfect for him. He met the qualifications, and the job was with a local company that he had long respected. Knowing that there would be many applicants, however, he realized that he needed to find an internal contact. He knew that was the only way to stand out amid what would be strong competition for a job advertised so widely.

After racking his brain, he remembered that his neighbor Steve had once worked for the firm. Although Steve had left the company a few years back, Kevin suspected he might still have contacts there. With a printout of the job in hand, Kevin crossed the street and rang Steve's doorbell.

"Hi, Steve," said Kevin. "I just found this opening with XZ Corporation on the Internet. Didn't you work for them a while back?"

"I sure did," answered Steve. "I left about three years ago."

"This job seems like a really good match for my skills, and I've applied online," said Kevin. "I know that the competition will be fierce, and I'd like to find someone internal. Do you still know anyone there who might have any insight into this job?"

"I still have quite a few friends back there, so let me see what I can do," answered Steve. "Give me a couple of days, and I'll get back to you."

A couple of days later, Steve appeared at Kevin's door. He held a piece of paper is his hand with a woman's name and phone number written on it. His message was brief.

"This woman is a friend of mine. She is also the supervisor for the job you are interested in. I told her about you and she wants to talk to you. Call her."

Kevin was ecstatic. This break was even better than he had dared hope for! He thanked Steve profusely and immediately picked up the phone to call the contact Steve had given him.

———————————◯———————————

Other Search Methods

Whether They Work and When to Use Them

To beat your competition and land the perfect job, you must stretch beyond your comfort level and try search strategies that most job hunters either don't try or don't execute correctly. Some of these approaches will be very different and uncomfortable for you, but you must make the effort. You never know where that next job lead will come from; attempting some new approaches could make the difference between a couple months of unemployment and a year of it.

One common mistake job seekers make is dismissing outright new strategies because of someone else's experience. Just because your neighbor attended a job fair and found it worthless doesn't mean that you will have the same experience. Another alumnus of your university may have tried the alumni career services office and found it lacking, but your visit could turn out completely different. You *must* try everything at your disposal despite any editorializing by your friends and family. Let's take a look at some alternative job search approaches and how to best utilize them in your job search.

MARY ATTENDS A JOB FAIR

Mary opened the morning newspaper and was thrilled to see an announcement of a job fair to be held the following week. Sponsored by the local chamber of commerce, the job fair would be free of charge and open to the entire community. The article also mentioned the anticipated participation of about one hundred local companies. *This is great,* thought Mary. *All those employers in one place—how convenient that will be. This will be a big boost to my job search!* Mary closed the newspaper and made a note in her calendar to attend the job fair the following week.

Mary prepared to leave the house on the morning of the job fair. *It's going to be so big, with so much walking,* she thought. *I'd better wear my comfortable tennis shoes and dress in my sweat suit. That way I'll be able to see as many employers as possible and still be comfortable.* Mary quickly dressed and headed out the door. When she arrived at the job fair, she was surprised to see many people dressed very professionally in business suits. *How silly they are,* she thought. *They will be so uncomfortable by the end of the day!*

Mary wandered the floor of the job fair wondering which recruiter she should talk with first. There were so many employers! Finally, she randomly approached one of the employer booths. With a broad smile she shook the recruiter's hand and introduced herself.

"Hi, I'm Mary," she said. "I've been unemployed for several weeks, and I really need a job. What sorts of jobs are you hiring for?" As she introduced herself, Mary sensed a slight frown on the recruiter's mouth. *What in the world is that about?* she thought to herself. *Could it be because I don't have on one of those ridiculous business suits and dress shoes? At least I'm comfortable!*

"Well," responded the recruiter, "that really depends on what your qualifications are. Could I take a look at a copy of your résumé?" Mary was flabbergasted. Wasn't the reason for the job fair for her to find out what kinds of opportunities the employers had available? And now this guy wanted her résumé to find out about her! "I'm sorry," answered Mary. "I didn't bring any résumés with me today. I didn't think I would need them. Can't you just tell me what jobs you have open?" "Thanks anyway," answered the recruiter, "but I'd better move on to the next person in line."

HOW SHOULD YOU HANDLE A JOB FAIR?

First off, let's define exactly what a job fair is. A job fair is an event where a group of employers come together in a central space (often a hotel ballroom or convention center) and set up tables and booths, much like a trade show. Job hunters circulate through the event and target employers they are interested in. Short conversations are held between the recruiters and the applicants, and decisions are usually made on the spot about which candidates will be followed up with. Job fairs can be very general (sponsored by a metropolitan newspaper or chamber of commerce), sponsored by a university for its students and alumni, or sponsored for a specific career field (often by a professional association).

Almost universally, job hunters approach job fairs with apprehension, and sometimes dread. The sad truth is that most job hunters don't have the slightest idea how to prepare for or work a job fair effectively. Since decisions about whether to interview are often made on the spot at a job fair, your preparation and approach on the day of the job fair will make all the difference in the world.

How Do You Prepare for a Job Fair?

If you actually do prepare you will already be ahead. Most of your competition will simply show up. The basics are similar to preparing for an interview:

○ Do you have appropriate business attire? Are your shoes shined? Does your hair need to be cut/styled?

○ Do you have sufficient copies of your résumé printed on good quality paper? Take double the number of copies that you think you will need.

○ Have you prepared and practiced your one-minute commercial until you are totally comfortable with it?

○ If there are specific employers you know you want to speak with, have you done some research on them ahead of time?

If you can get the names ahead of time of companies that will be represented at the job fair, you can plan ahead to maximize your time. If a map is available (and one often is available online before the job fair), you can even scope out a route to the employers in which you are most interested. The most popular employers will likely have long lines of people eager to speak with them. You may spend substantial amounts of time waiting in line. Having identified the employers you are most interested in, and even mapped out your path to reach them, will help you to maximize the time you have available.

What Should You Do on the Day of the Job Fair?

Dress professionally! In my days as a recruiter, I saw way too many job fair attendees show up in jeans, T-shirts, and other kinds of casual wear. Because your time speaking with a recruiter will be short, first impressions are *even more* important than usual, and a major part of a first impression is how you look. You should go to the job fair dressed as if you were going to a job interview. Any interaction with a recruiter will be prefaced by a positive first impression based on appearance.

Plan to arrive as early as possible to be there when the job fair doors open. You may be able to reach one or two of the more popular employers before the lengthy lines build up. Employers will also be more likely to remember someone who makes a good impression early in the day because they too get tired as the day wears on!

Attend the job fair *alone*! Too many job hunters seek the security of friends or colleagues when they are faced with the stress of attending a job fair. They travel in "packs" through the job fair, appearing at employer booths together. Recruiters find that talking with such a group makes it almost impossible for any one person to stand out, and they may question your independence and self-reliance if their first interaction with you requires the support of several friends. Having a crowd may give you a sense of security in a stressful situation, but it won't help you score points with a recruiter.

Stick to your plan! Walking into a job fair (especially a large one) can be daunting. Even with a plan, you may be tempted to start wandering randomly and focusing only on the companies that have the shortest lines. You may talk to more recruiters that way, but are you really talking with the ones you should be focusing on? Keep to your plan, even if it means making fewer contacts. This is a situation where quality is more important than quantity.

Be prepared to present yourself professionally and concisely. Job fairs tend to be very crowded in tough economic times, and your opportunity to make a good impression will be very brief. Your one-minute commercial is critical in this situation because it is a great way of telling a recruiter who you are and what you're about. If you've researched the company, what can you also tell the recruiter about how your skills could contribute to the organization? Most of your competitors will simply thrust a résumé into the recruiter's face and talk about how they "really need a job." One recruiter in northern Virginia recently noted that out of more than one hundred applicants she and her colleagues met at a job fair, only four received follow-up interviews. Your brief encounter with each recruiter is your chance to shine, but you really must take full advantage of the opportunity!

How Should You Follow Up After the Job Fair?

If you can get a business card from a recruiter, that will give you a follow-up strategy. Most recruiters at job fairs are stingy with business cards and only distribute them if there is some interest in the candidate. If you are able to obtain a business card, be sure to follow up within twenty-four hours with a short thank-you note. Doing so will get your name in front of the recruiter one more time, perhaps encouraging him or her to take another look at your résumé. At the very least a note shows you have good manners!

If a recruiter provides you with any kind of application paperwork to complete, do so immediately and thoroughly. Many application forms are long and cumbersome, and applicants typically avoid dealing with them as long as they can. Time is of the essence immediately following the job fair, so don't delay! Also be sure that you are neat and thorough. Many sets of application materials are rejected simply because they are incomplete, illegible, or filled with inaccuracies. In a tough job market you have to pay attention to every little detail!

HOW CAN YOU MOST EFFECTIVELY RESPOND TO NEWSPAPER ADS?

Even in this era of the Internet, most major newspapers continue to publish a classified "help wanted" section. The same ads are typically on the newspaper websites, but some people find it easier just to pick up the newspaper from their driveways and review the ads. In addition, many local and weekly newspapers also have a more localized "help wanted" section. Employers may utilize smaller newspapers to appeal to a more narrow geographic market or to save on print advertising costs. These smaller newspapers may not have an online presence, so it's worth taking a look at the print edition.

The same rules apply to responding to newspaper job ads as to online postings. Be sure to read the ad carefully and identify the major skill sets the employer is seeking. Customize both your résumé and cover letter to ensure that those skills are mentioned, along with evidence of expertise. Try to find an inside contact who will be able to champion your cause!

HOW CAN YOU USE COLLEGE AND UNIVERSITY CAREER SERVICES OFFICES?

Most college and university career services offices offer some level of service to their alumni. Some large universities even staff a career services office exclusively for alumni. The majority of alumni don't take advantage of these services, and they are often quite good. Any services offered to you as an alum should be counted among your tools in a tough market.

Services from Your College or University

The level of services offered to alumni varies from school to school. Some offer the same comprehensive services that are available to current students. Others offer access to a career counselor and job listings but only limited access to on-campus interviews. Many schools have at least a career counselor who specializes in alumni. Call the career services office of any school from which you received a degree. Ask what specific services are available for alumni. (Many schools also list this information on their websites.) If a career counselor is available to meet with alumni, make an appointment and meet with that person. Such counselors will likely have a strong knowledge of the local job market, particularly for the fields in which the school awards degrees or has a particular reputation for excellence.

Services from a Distance

It's entirely likely that you live nowhere near any of the schools from which you earned your degrees. Many schools will still be able to provide you with a limited suite of services. These sometimes include lists of open positions e-mailed to you on a regular basis or telephone counseling with a career counselor. Although these options are often not as effective as in-person services, take full advantage of whatever is offered.

Many schools also have reciprocity agreements. That means that your school will provide services to alumni of other schools if those schools are willing to do the same for alumni of your school. Make a list of the colleges and universities in your current area; then call the career services office at the school from which you graduated and ask about reciprocity for services with the schools on your list. You will often be able to obtain at least limited services from a school located near you.

How Can You Use Your College/University Alumni Association?

Almost every school has an alumni association. Your alumni association can be a valuable resource in connecting you with other alumni in either your geographic area or career field. Some schools provide online alumni directories, and others operate some form of referral service. If you are really lucky, your school has solicited its alumni for volunteers open to helping recent grads or other alumni. Whatever the level of service, you should be able to tap into a network of fellow alumni who can be rich resources.

Because many alumni have warm feelings about their alma mater, they are open to helping fellow graduates. Don't necessarily anticipate a job offer, but expect someone who may be willing to sit down with you and share his or her knowledge of the career field and job market. That person may also be willing to connect you with people in his or her network who might be helpful to you. As in any networking situation, be on the lookout for ways that you can reciprocate any help that is offered and build a solid networking relationship.

I serve as a volunteer for the career services office at the college where I received my undergraduate degree. Students and alumni can get my contact information and get in touch with me if they want more information about job hunting in the Washington, D.C., area. In the past I've helped people better customize their résumés for this market and have provided advice about how to look for leads and contacts in this area.

HOW SHOULD YOU USE PRIVATE SEARCH FIRMS/ EMPLOYMENT AGENCIES?

Search firms and employment agencies should also be a part of your comprehensive job search strategy. There are several different types of firms/agencies, however, and you need to make sure that you are working with a firm that will be in the best position to help in your search. Some specialize in particular career fields or industries. They can be helpful because they're likely to have more extensive contacts or information in a specific field/industry. You need to know, however, that there is no regulation of this industry, and not all search firms are ethical. Your best option is to ask for recommendations from friends or colleagues who have used a firm in the past. If you can't get a personal recommendation, you can check on retained search firms by looking for membership in the Association of Executive Search Consultants. You may also find it useful to ask the following questions:

○ How much experience does the firm have?
○ What is the firm's placement record?
○ Does the firm focus on particular specialties (e.g., accounting, human resources, legal)? A firm specializing in your career field may be better prepared to work with you.

○ What services does the firm offer? Will it help you prepare for interviews or polish your résumé?

○ Who will work with you directly as your "counselor"? Ask to meet that person to establish your comfort level with him or her.

With any kind of search firm or employment agency, don't expect your point of contact to be a full-fledged career counselor or to conduct your job search for you. One of my clients recently insisted that using agencies was "the" way to find a job. She registered with several and then settled back to wait. Given the tough economy, she was called for only a couple of interviews, both for jobs she didn't want. Eventually she realized that her job search would have to consist of more than waiting for an agency to find her a job—but by that point she had lost valuable time.

Search firms and employment agencies are businesses, not career counselors. Because in most cases the firms are paid by employers, they tend to look out for the best interests of the employer, not the job seeker. If you have unusual or hard-to-find skills, you will probably get lots of attention. If many other applicants share your skill sets, you may get little or no attention. Just be aware of what a search firm's priorities are, and think of their services as just one tool in your job search arsenal.

Because a small percentage of firms are less than scrupulous, be careful when you register with a firm. If any of the following warning signs appear, head for the door:

○ The firm asks for either a registration fee or finder's fee. (Never pay either!)

○ The representative insists that you must sign the contract on the spot after your initial meeting with the firm. (You should be given the time to read the contract carefully before you sign it and perhaps even have legal counsel review it.)

○ The firm demands that you sign exclusively with them. (Although I don't advocate signing with large numbers of firms, signing an exclusivity clause limits you from working with *any* other firms.)

For our purposes, we'll look at the types of firms in four different categories:

o General employment agencies
o Contingency agencies
o Retained search firms
o Temporary (temp) agencies

You should be certain you understand what type of firm you will be working with before you sign on the dotted line.

General Employment Agencies

Traditional employment agencies are typically used to fill relatively low-level or hourly jobs. Some are paid fees by the employer they are recruiting for, and some charge the job seeker an up-front fee. I don't recommend working with an agency that charges an up-front fee. If the fees are employer-paid, beware of pressure to accept a job for which you have been referred. Because the agency is paid only for a successful placement, it is in their interest that you accept any job offered to you. Of course, any decision about accepting an offer must be yours and yours alone. You should never accept a job just because it is offered to you!

Contingency Agencies

Contingency agencies are typically used for mid-level jobs, and the employer always pays the fee. The fee is still based, however, on the successful placement of a candidate. No placement = no fee! Because of this, the better contingency firms will take the time to understand both the employer's needs and the candidate's fit for the position. They may refer just one or several candidates based on the available pool and the relationship with the employer, but the incentive is to get one of their candidates placed.

Retained Search Firms

Retained search firms typically focus on executive-level jobs. The employer pays a flat fee for the search and often gives the firm exclusive rights to conduct the search for a specific period of time. The search firm is paid regardless of whether it fills the position. Retained firms tend to work from a "short list" and typically refer only a handful of well-qualified applicants to the employer. If you register with a retained search firm, assume that you will be referred for positions only if you are highly qualified.

Temporary (Temp) Agencies

Temporary (temp) agencies fill jobs on a short-term or contractual basis. With some firms you will actually be an employee of the temp agency; with others you will be a temporary employee of the firm to which you are referred. Some temp agencies even offer a limited benefits package if you are directly employed by them. In either case, there is no long-term commitment for either you or the company at which you work.

Many job seekers are reluctant to use temp firms, fearing that they will get "stuck" in a temp job that will interfere with their search for a "real" job. The secret that many job hunters don't know is that in a tough economy many employers take a "temp-to-perm" approach in their hiring. By hiring an employee first as a temp, they get to take a "test-drive" and see how he or she fits into the organization. After a few weeks or months of successful performance, the temporary employee is frequently converted to a full-time employee.

There are several other advantages to accepting temporary opportunities while pursuing your job search:

○ You can try out a variety of opportunities and employers without a long-term commitment.
○ If the position is "temp to perm," you can evaluate the company from the inside and whether is it right for you.

- You can get an inside track on unadvertised positions within the company where you are temping.
- You may be able to develop some new skills and enhance your résumé.
- Your network of contacts and colleagues will expand.

Because temporary opportunities and use of a "temp-to-perm" approach tend to be more common in a bad economy, you really should consider registering with a couple of temp agencies as part of your approach. Even an assignment that doesn't turn into something permanent can provide you with some much-needed income and a boost of self-esteem.

COMMUNITY OR GOVERNMENT AGENCIES

Depending on where you live, there may be a range of community and government agencies that provide job search assistance, often free of charge. Government agencies range from large state employment agencies to smaller "one-stop" centers on the county or city level. Many job seekers have traditionally avoided such agencies, thinking that the jobs and services were targeted toward very low-level jobs.

In reality, most government agencies work with a wide variety of employers, helping them fill a range of jobs. Some agencies even have job developers on their staffs whose sole responsibility is to prospect for job openings in the local area. With the advent of "one-stop" career centers in many areas, the level of services offered and job listings provided has increased significantly beyond the stereotype.

If you wish to be assisted by a government agency, you will typically be asked to attend an orientation session providing an overview of the services provided. You will then be assigned a counselor to work with on your job search. Be forewarned that counselors in most government agencies are very overworked and carry large caseloads. To make the most of their time and attention, it is critical that you follow up on any requests or assignments they give you. The level of service they are able to provide will be far better if you are an active coparticipant with them in the job search process. Don't expect a counselor from a government agency to "find" a job for you but rather to partner with you in the search.

In addition to government agencies and services, many community agencies are aimed at particular segments of the population. For example, an organization called "40Plus" is targeted at assisting job seekers more than forty years of age. Other community agencies are designed to assist specific ethnic groups. If you do find a community agency targeting a niche that you fit, be sure to take advantage of the resources. They will be able to zero in on issues unique to your niche that you may be dealing with, such as age discrimination, and will have lots of helpful advice and techniques for handling those issues.

KEVIN VISITS HIS COUNTY EMPLOYMENT CENTER

During a visit to his local library, Kevin picked up a pamphlet describing the employment services available to residents of his area. On the list of agencies was the address and phone number for the local "one-stop" agency serving his county. *I know I need to turn over every stone,* thought Kevin, *so I guess I should really check this out.*

The next morning, Kevin called the number listed in the pamphlet for the "one stop." When the receptionist answered the phone, Kevin explained that he was interested in finding out what kinds of services the agency could offer to him. The receptionist told him about an upcoming orientation he would need to attend in order to access the services offered by the center. *That's kind of a nuisance,* thought Kevin, *but if that's their policy I guess I can go along with it.* He booked himself into the next orientation session.

Kevin arrived for the orientation session with mixed expectations. He had heard that these "one-stop" centers were focused primarily on lower-tier jobs than he was looking for, but he knew it was worth a shot. As he looked around the room, he was surprised to see a real mix of people from all walks of life. A young woman came into the front of the room and opened the orientation session. Kevin was surprised to hear the scope of services available and to find out that he would be assigned a counselor to work with him on his job search. Maybe this "one-stop" center would turn out to be an asset in his job search plan after all!

PART 3

The Interview and Beyond

So . . . after all the hard work of the job search, you've landed an interview. Congratulations! The journey isn't over yet, but getting the opportunity for an interview is a big step forward. It's still up to you to make the most of this opportunity and prove that you are the best person for the job. The chapters in this part will take you through the entire interview process:

○ Preparation
○ Staying cool during your interview
○ Following up afterward

Effective and thorough preparation is critical to the success of your interview. In a tough job market employers expect candidates to be well prepared for often challenging interview situations and questions. A candidate who is well prepared for an interview will likely equate to an employee well prepared to do the job.

As prepared as you may be, the unexpected often happens during the interview process. A question comes up for which you are totally unprepared, or you walk into an interview room and unexpectedly find a panel of five interviewers ready to fire questions at you. How you handle the unexpected and keep your cool often makes or breaks your success during the interview.

In a tough economy, follow-up is everything. Many of your competitors will do no follow-up at all after an interview, so what you do after the interview is over is critical. Something as mundane as a thank-you note or letter could be the difference between getting or not getting the job. You *must* follow up if you want to seal the deal.

Preparation

Taking Charge of How They See You

One of the biggest mistakes I see clients make is walking into the interview unprepared. Whether it's their failure to prepare for questions they might be asked or not doing advance research about the employer, the interview is bound to go badly if they haven't done their homework up front. Many candidates simply don't bother!

You *must* be well prepared when you walk in the door for your interview. *Everything* you do leading up to the actual interview can make it or break it. From making sure you have the logistics under control (time, travel, etc.) to preparing for questions you may be asked, you must do a comprehensive job of preparing. Let's take a look at some of the types of preparation you absolutely must do.

MARY LANDS ANOTHER INTERVIEW

After weeks and weeks of job searching and following her interview for the commission-only job, Mary finally landed a legitimate interview. She was thrilled. The interview was with a growing local firm, and the position description sounded perfect for Mary's skill sets. She knew that she must make the best of this opportunity.

The day before the interview, Mary decided to do some preparation. *Hmmm . . . ,* she thought, *I wonder what I should wear? I know that the company is quite conservative, but I also know that I need to make an impression. I think that I will wear my bright pink suit. That should really stand out and shake up that stodgy place.*

Mary next considered some of the questions she might be asked. She knew some of the standards included "Tell me about yourself." and "What is your biggest weakness?" *I really want this job,* she thought, *so I'd better make up some really good answers for the questions I might be asked. If they ask about weaknesses, I'll just tell them I can't think of any. They certainly aren't going to be interested in a candidate who has a whole bunch of weaknesses to talk about.*

Finally, Mary thought about how she would travel to the interview. *I know that company is over on Glide Street,* she thought. *I'm not sure exactly where . . . it's a pretty long street, but I'll figure it out. After all, what's the worst thing that could happen? I might be a few minutes late. I'm sure that happens with candidates all the time.* With that, Mary moved on to other things, confident that she was prepared for her interview the next day.

STEP ONE: KNOW YOURSELF

This first step in preparing for an interview starts long before you walk in the door. Go back to Chapter 1 and review the worksheets you completed analyzing your technical and transferable skills. Can you provide concrete examples from your past for each of your skill sets? Review the job description for the skills critical for the position for which you are interviewing. How do they match your skills, and what examples illustrate that? If skills that you don't possess are included in the job description, can you demonstrate how you have used similar or related skill sets?

Now is also the time to go back and review the one-minute commercials that you developed in Chapter 2. You should have developed one about technical skills and one about transferable skills. Are you happy with your one-minute commercials, or do they need to be refined further? Have you practiced them in front of family, colleagues, or friends? What kind of feedback did you get? Do they flow off your tongue in a natural conversational tone? You should continue to perfect and practice your one-minute commercials as part of your interview preparation process.

STEP TWO: YOUR VERY FIRST IMPRESSION

When do you think the first impression happens? Is it when you greet the receptionist when you walk in the front door for your interview? Is it the handshake when you first meet the interviewer(s)? Actually, first impressions begin long before then and are a critical part of your interview preparation.

One could argue that the first impression really begins with your résumé. In most cases your résumé is the very first contact an employer has with you. If you've made it to the interview, you've obviously passed the résumé test, but you should still be aware that employers do form impressions the very first time they read your résumé. Does it really represent you in the manner you want? You know by now that it's never "complete," so continue to make revisions as you need to. Be particularly attentive to any feedback you receive from a potential employer. One important note—be sure to keep track of which version of your résumé is submitted to each employer!

Every interaction, both personal and virtual, that you have with a potential employer is critical. For example, does your e-mail address reflect a professional image? "Hot Stuff 2009@ . . ." is not going to make the impression you would like. Also consider the message on your voicemail. One client of mine used his four-year-old daughter for his voicemail greeting on his home telephone. Although her voice may be cute for relatives and personal friends to hear, the image it projected was not a professional one. Be sure your voicemail greeting is professional-sounding and concise.

Maintain a professional tone in all of your e-mail and phone interactions in advance of the interview. Treat relevant e-mails the way you would other professional business correspondence. That means proofing each e-mail very carefully for spelling and grammar before sending it. You should also eliminate your use of emoticons—the little smiley faces and other symbols made with various keyboard combinations. Many of us use them frequently in personal e-mails to friends and family, but they aren't appropriate for corresponding with a prospective employer.

Any telephone conversations with a potential employer should be professional and courteous. The conversation is a business conversation and should be treated as such. Consider the situation of one applicant who found himself lost on the way to his interview, despite using a map provided by the employer. He called the prospective employer and reached the administrative assistant. He proceeded to verbally blast her, accusing her of trying to sabotage his interview. Needless to say, his interview (for a customer service position requiring the ability to interact well under stress) might as well have been over before it even began.

STEP THREE: PRACTICAL LOGISTICS

Have you ever heard the old saying "It's the small things that always get you!"? Such is often the case with interviewing. Lack of attention to the basic logistics can ruin your chances before the interview even begins. Not preparing your clothing ahead of time or ignoring transportation issues until the morning of your interview can result in disaster.

Settle on Clothing for Your Interview

Plan in advance what you will wear for your interview. Make sure that your clothing is appropriate for the setting as well as neatly cleaned and pressed. An interviewer will expect you to be at your best on the day of the interview, so inappropriate or dirty clothing will cause concern about what will happen when you're not at your best.

What types of clothing are appropriate for interviews? In general terms, plan to dress at least one level above what people wear when they go to work in that environment. For most professional positions that will mean conservative business attire. For a factory or blue-collar position, it may mean a neat pair of pants and shirt. Finding out what people typically wear to work in the environment in which you are interviewing will help you better gauge how you should dress.

Here are some specific suggestions for women and men interviewing for professional level positions:

Women

○ Wear a conservative business suit in muted colors. Bright colors or clothing that is better suited for a social setting will not make as good an impression.

○ Whether to wear a skirt or pants depends on how conservative the environment is at the interviewing organization. Pants are generally not a good idea for an interview at an extremely conservative organization.

○ Wear conservative, close-toed shoes. Some interviewers report an epidemic of candidates who were otherwise well dressed showing up for interviews wearing flip-flops. Don't wear footwear for an interview that's meant for the beach!

○ Use only light makeup and wear minimal jewelry. The focus needs to be on the professional you during the interview.

○ Avoid perfume completely. Interviews are often held in small rooms, and even light perfume can quickly permeate. Some people are also allergic.

Men

○ Wear a conservative business suit, white shirt, and conservative tie if interviewing for a professional position. Better to err on the side of being overdressed for the interview.

○ Use dark socks and well-shined dress shoes. It's amazing how many men I've seen ruin a nice suit by wearing white socks! And some interviewers (especially if they are retired military) make a judgment by how well the shoes are shined.

○ Don't wear cologne or aftershave. The smell can permeate a small interview room, and some people are allergic.

○ Get a conservative haircut, if you don't have one already. If you do, get a trim.

One interview candidate woke up early on the morning of his interview and dressed in the early morning light. He had retrieved his two blue suits from the dry cleaner the day before, and put one of them on. Later, as he drove to his interview, he happened to glance down at his pants and at the suit coat on the seat next to him. He realized to his horror that they didn't match! The dry cleaner had mixed the coats and pants from the two suits.

The moral of this story: Carefully check your clothing *before* the day of the interview!

Prepare Your Materials

You won't want to take a bulging briefcase to your interview, but you'll need to carry a portfolio or clean folder with several items the interviewer might ask for or need.

- Several copies of your résumé (at least enough for you and all who will be interviewing you)
- Several copies of your list of references
- Your "short list" of questions to ask

If you work in a creative field or a field where an employer might want to see writing samples, be sure to bring along several representative samples of your work in a portfolio. Don't bring originals—copies are best, in case you are asked to leave the samples behind for future review.

Get to the Interview on Time

Another important part of your planning is deciding how you are going to get to the interview, and planning to arrive early. Rushing in at the very last minute is just as bad as being late. Waiting until the day of the interview to consider which route you will drive or what bus or subway you will take is a recipe for disaster!

If you are going to an unfamiliar location, this is more than just mapping out your route to get there. Consider making a test run at the same time of day you'll be traveling to your interview. You never know what traffic or other transportation issues might come up at that specific time of day.

One of my clients made a test run to her interview location, although not at the time of day her interview was scheduled. On the day of her interview, she left her home with what she thought was plenty of time to spare. What she didn't plan on was the very long and slow freight train crossing the road on her way to the interview. Although she made it on time, it was a close call. She later learned that the same train regularly blocked the crossing at about the same time every day.

STEP FOUR: PREPARING FOR INTERVIEW QUESTIONS

Every interview comes with a wide range of questions. Often it will include a number of standard questions for which you can effectively prepare. Others are more technical or job-specific and are more difficult to anticipate. Doing as much preparation as you can possibly do, however, is the key to succeeding. Your competition may be left fumbling for adequate answers to the most basic questions if they haven't prepared. In a tough job market, your advance preparation can make the difference.

First, you must know the content of your résumé. Have a good handle on the skills and strengths you have to offer, and think about how you can compensate for the areas that aren't strengths. It's critical that you know your résumé backward and forward. You will almost always be asked about the content (sometimes in great detail), and you need to be prepared to provide concrete examples and answers.

A number of standard interview questions are likely to come up during almost any interview but especially during initial screening interviews. A list of many standard questions is included at the end of this chapter. You should not practice the answers until you sound like a robot, but you should understand the questions well enough to be able to provide lucid answers with as many specific examples as possible.

One way to prepare for standard questions is to consider them from the viewpoint of the interviewer. Why, exactly, is the interviewer asking the question, and what does he or she hope to accomplish? Is the interviewer asking, "Tell me about yourself?" because it is important to know everything about your personal life, or is he or she interested in a short overview of your experience, skills, and strengths? Trying to piece together why questions are being asked will help you better develop an answer that gives the interviewer what he or she needs and wants. Later in this chapter you'll find an overview of the most common questions from the interviewer's viewpoint.

To prepare for more detailed or job-specific questions, examine the job description or announcement for the job for which you are interviewing. Skills or strengths that you see repeated more than once or that are mentioned prominently in the description are likely to be good fodder for interview questions. Consider carefully those skills and strengths, and develop specific examples of how you've used or displayed them in the past.

STEP FIVE: RESEARCH

You must research any organization with which you will be interviewing. Researching used to mean a trip to the public library to dig through massive directories. With the advent of the Internet, the research task has become far easier, but it also has become even more expected of candidates. Since the information is so readily available, there is no excuse for not having an understanding of the organization you are interviewing with and its products or services.

Your basic research should involve digging through the organization's website and reviewing its annual report if it is available. You don't need to know every last detail about the business (e.g., they manufactured 3,756,850 widgets last year), but you should have a good general understanding of what the business is about and who the customers are.

If you are interviewing with a government agency or a nonprofit organization, you should also have a basic understanding of what it is all about. How does the government agency fit into the larger government structure, and what are its priorities? What is the mission of the nonprofit organization, and what constituencies does it serve? It's critical to most government organizations and nonprofits that you understand their mission and goals and be on board with them.

STEP SIX: THE DAY OF THE INTERVIEW

The final part of your interview preparation involves what you do on the actual interview day. You can still make some key mistakes before you get into the interview room that can doom your chances for a successful interview. Here are a few definite dos:

- **It may seem like common sense, but get a good night's sleep before your interview.** The more rested you are, the more likely you will be alert and ready to deal with the toughest of questions. Many recruiters have more than one story about candidates who weren't well rested and committed all kinds of errors, up to and including falling asleep during the interview!

- **Be sure to take along several copies of your résumé.** Although everyone interviewing you should have received it in advance, files do get lost. You show your preparedness by having several copies with you if they are needed.

- **You should also take along several copies of your list of references.** If an interview goes well, the employer may want to move to the next step by calling some of your references. Having a neatly prepared document with their names, addresses, phone numbers, and e-mail addresses also shows your preparedness. Letters of reference are fine for documentation, but most employers will want to actually call and speak with your references to ask specific questions about your skills and background. Your references should be people who know you professionally (not your relative or next-door neighbor) who can address your skills and qualifications. Be sure you've *asked* each of your references (at least three) if they are willing to serve as a reference for you. You should also supply each with an updated copy of your résumé so they can field questions if necessary

○ **Another commonsense item is to use a breath mint just before you go into the interview room.** This is especially important if you are a cigarette smoker. Interview rooms are often small. You may not be aware of your bad breath, but it could have a negative impact on the interviewer.

KEVIN LANDS AN INTERVIEW

Kevin's very persistent job search efforts had paid off. After several weeks of looking, he had landed an interview for a very good job with a reputable local company. He was excited about the prospect of meeting with the interviewer and proving that he had the skills and ambition to excel in the new job.

Kevin knew, however, that he first needed to make sure that he was well prepared to take advantage of the opportunity. He had a good idea of what skill sets he would likely be asked about, and also knew that several traditional interview questions would probably come up. How could he best get ready?

After a little bit of thought he decided to call his friend Stan. Stan worked in human resources for a large local firm and would probably be able to provide good advice. He called and quickly got Stan on the phone.

"Hi, Stan," said Kevin. "I have great news! I've landed an interview with that new firm on the other side of town. I'm really excited!"

"That's great," answered Stan. "Do you feel like you're prepared for the interview?"

"Funny you should ask," said Kevin. "That's exactly what I was calling you for advice on. What would you suggest doing to prepare?"

"Why don't you come in tomorrow and we'll do a mock interview," answered Stan. "If you can give me an idea of some of the types of questions you're likely to be asked, I can practice them with you and give some feedback."

Kevin went to Stan's office the next day for the mock interview. Stan asked several questions that Kevin thought might come up in the interview but also added several of his own. Kevin excelled in answering some of them but struggled with others. Stan gave constructive feedback and suggestions, some of which Kevin had never considered. As he left Stan's office, Kevin thought to himself, *That was a really helpful exercise. I feel much better prepared and less nervous now!*

COMMON INTERVIEW QUESTIONS

The questions below are a partial list of what you might be asked during an interview. These common questions are most frequently used during initial screening interviews. The list is by no means exhaustive, and similar questions could be asked with slightly different wording. The questions are roughly organized according to categories of interest/possible interview format. Think through and practice these questions ahead of time, particularly those that you think may give you trouble.

Icebreakers

These are designed to put you at ease, while at the same time seeing how well you engage in an informal conversation. Depending on the type of position for which you are interviewing (e.g., sales), your ability to make "small talk" could be part of the interview process.

- Were the directions to get here easy to follow?
- Isn't this weather great (horrible)?
- Did you see the big game over the weekend?

Education/Career

These questions will assess your educational and career backgrounds, and what kind of a "fit" they are for the position. As you talk about your background and skills, you'll want to give specific examples and relate them as much as possible to the job for which you are interviewing.

- Tell me about yourself.
- Tell me about your last job.
- Tell me about the best boss you ever had. The worst.
- Tell me about your educational background.
- Why did you choose your college/graduate school major or degree?
- Where do you see yourself in your career in five years? Ten years?
- How do you define success?
- What accomplishments have you found you enjoyed most in your career?

Background/Skills/Experience

These questions will delve into the specifics of what you can offer the prospective employer. If the position requires very specific or technical skills, expect very detailed questions probing your expertise in those skills. These questions may also be behavioral questions requiring you to cite specific examples in your answer of how you displayed the trait or skill in a past situation.

- What are your strengths? Weaknesses?
- How would you describe your managerial style? Your leadership style?
- Describe a managerial situation in which you had to make a decision without all the information you needed. How did you make the decision?

○ What experience have you had hiring employees? What about firing employees?
○ How do you handle stress?
○ Describe a situation where you had to juggle multiple priorities. How did you do it, and were you successful?
○ How important was communication in your last job?
○ Describe a time when you had to be an effective team player.
○ What is your experience in handling budgets?
○ What was your biggest success? Biggest failure?

Closing/Procedural

As the interview nears its end, the interviewer will usually let you know that he or she is finished and end with some closing or procedural questions. In most cases, there will be an opportunity for you to ask a few questions. A good interviewer will tell you what the time line is and next steps are, but be sure to ask if this information isn't provided.

○ Why should I hire you?
○ What is your availability to begin work if you are offered this position?
○ Is there any other information about you that I should have?
○ What are your salary expectations?
○ Do you have any questions?

Possible Questions for You to Ask the Interviewer
○ Can you describe the "corporate culture" of this organization?
○ Does this position/department have its own budget? Who controls it?
○ Where does this position/department fit into the company's organizational structure?
○ Who will make the final hiring decision for this position?
○ Are training/professional development opportunities supported by this organization?
○ How is performance measured in this organization?

Questions *Not* to Ask the Interviewer

- What is the salary?
- When can I take my first vacation?
- How old are you?

STANDARD INTERVIEW QUESTIONS: THE EMPLOYER'S POINT OF VIEW

The best way to understand some of the most common standard interview questions is to understand the employer's point of view, and why the questions are being asked. Here are a few of the most standard questions, and the rationale behind asking them:

- **Tell me about yourself.** Recruiters ask this question for several reasons. They may want to see how you react to a very broad question. This question is totally unstructured, and they want to see how you are able to build a structure with your answer. They may also want to see how you can concisely and articulately build an answer. This gives them an idea of how you can condense and deliver important information.

   Your best approach is to be well prepared with your one-minute commercial. You'll show that you can deliver a well-structured answer to an unstructured question in a concise and articulate way, while providing only pertinent information.

- **Where do you see yourself/your career in five years?** This question is commonly asked both to get an idea of your level of ambition and also your sense of reality. Telling the recruiter that you want to be CEO of the company may seem cute but will raise questions about your grasp on reality. Saying that you hope to still be working away in the job you are interviewing for may give the impression that you aren't very ambitious. Best to think about what career paths are realistic for you and how that relates to possible future options in their organization.

- **What is your biggest weakness?** The recruiter probably isn't really all that interested in what your weakness is. Rather, this question is about attitude. Do you discuss your weakness in a way that shows you don't expect to overcome it, or do you talk about what you've been doing to overcome something that you perceive as a weakness? The latter shows that you have a "can-do" attitude and won't give up easily when faced with workplace challenges.

    To prepare for this question, identify an area for development that you are either currently working on or have addressed at some point in the past. Discuss why this "weakness" was important to you and what you've specifically done to address it. Your "can-do" attitude will come through.

- **What is your biggest strength?** The reverse of the weaknesses question, and you would think that this one would be easier for a candidate to answer, but it's usually not. Recruiters love this question because they can get a good idea as to whether an applicant is in touch with the skills necessary for the job and whether he or she has them. An applicant who knows what he or she brings to the table will probably be more self-confident and effective in the workplace. As an applicant, really think about your skills (strengths) that relate to the job and be prepared to describe them with specific examples.

- **How do you handle stress?** Most workplaces and jobs in the twenty-first century carry with them a substantial amount of stress. Employees who are most successful acknowledge that the stress exists and have a strategy for dealing with it. This question is designed to determine how effectively you handle a stressful environment. In answering it, you should consider exactly how to frame your coping strategies, and include examples of how you have handled the stress. Answers such as "I thrive on stress" aren't necessarily helpful. People who "thrive" on stress often burn out quickly. Employers usually look for employees who have a well-balanced approach to their work and lives. They generally handle stress much better.

○ **Why did you leave your last job?** Downsizing has become a way of life in recent years, and you may have lost your last job as a result. It's not something to be ashamed of—there is no longer a stigma attached. Many excellent employees have lost their jobs simply because of poor business conditions.

Because the question about why you left your last job is common, you do need to be prepared to handle it effectively. It's understandable to feel some bitterness about your previous employer and how they handled your termination, but this must absolutely not come through when you are in an interview. A potential employer might view your "sour grapes" as indicative of a negative attitude in general.

To make sure you are prepared to discuss the issue of why you left as positively as possible, you should develop a strategy in the form of an "exit statement." In an exit statement, you briefly outline why your previous employment was terminated. If possible, you should also mention something positive you gained from the past employer and/or the situation. This will demonstrate a good attitude and positive outlook. A possible exit statement might go something like this:

My employment with XYZ Corporation was terminated when a business decision was made to eliminate my division. Everyone who worked in my division lost their jobs as a result. I gained great experience at XYZ and hated to see my job end, but I also understand that it was purely a strategic decision on their part necessitated by the poor economy.

Just as you should practice your one-minute commercials until they flow naturally off your tongue, you should do the same with your exit statement.

Your Interview Preparation "To Do" List

○ Do you "know yourself" adequately?
- Have you reviewed your skills and strengths?
- Have you reviewed the content of your résumé?
- Have you practiced your one-minute commercial?

○ Have you ensured that you have made a good first impression *before* the interview?

○ Have you gotten all of the practical logistics in order?
- Have you prepared your interview clothing?
- Are your materials ready to take along?
- Is your transportation arranged?

○ Have you prepared for both standard and technical interview questions?

○ Have you researched the organization?

○ Are you prepared for the actual interview day?
- Have you made sure you'll be sufficiently rested?
- Do you have copies of your résumé?
- Do you have copies of your list of references?

Staying Cool

Handling the Unexpected During an Interview

In a competitive environment, every moment of the interview is critical. Any misstep can totally obscure all of your good answers. The unfortunate truth is that almost every interview includes an unexpected moment. A question arises that you aren't prepared for, or you are faced with an awkward situation. How you keep your cool and respond will make all the difference in the world in edging out your competition.

The day of your interview has arrived, and you feel totally prepared and ready to go. You're confident that you are going to present yourself well and ace this interview. Then, suddenly, the unexpected happens. Consider these real-life situations:

- The candidate arrives for the interview only to be told that his résumé is missing. Since he didn't bring a spare copy with him, could he please provide a "verbal" résumé? He panics wondering whether he can possibly remember everything written in his résumé.
- A second candidate nears the end of her interview confident that she has done well. She has answered the questions completely but concisely with good concrete examples. Suddenly, a question is asked and she is clueless about how to answer it. In fact, she isn't even clear on what the question means.

○ A third candidate arrives for her interview brimming with confidence. She smiles and chats with the receptionist who escorts her back to the interview room. When the door opens she sees not just one interviewer but a panel of six! Her heart sinks.

In this chapter we'll examine closely what happens during the actual interview process. What can go wrong, and what road-blocks can get in the way? We'll trace the structure of a typical interview and help you to see the process through the eyes of the employer.

MARY'S INTERVIEW

Mary was so excited! Following her previous interview disasters, she had landed another interview for a job that she really wanted. She was confident that she had the qualifications and looked forward to the opportunity to present them in a positive way. She had been told that she would be meeting with six different people on the day of the interview, but she was sure that she would be able to handle it.

On the day of the interview, Mary excitedly started the process with the first interviewer. She felt that she answered the questions articulately and also built a good rapport. As the day progressed, however, things started to go downhill.

As she entered the fifth interview, Mary realized that it was already mid-afternoon. *When is this going to be over?* she thought. *I am so tired. I really enjoyed that movie that I stayed up late watching last night, but I probably should have gotten to bed earlier. I had no idea this process would be so draining.*

The fifth interviewer entered the room and cheerfully introduced himself. Mary responded with a less than enthusiastic "nice to meet you," and the interview began.

The interviewer's first question was "Tell me about yourself, Mary." Every other interviewer had already asked Mary that same question, and she was tired of answering it. "Look," said the exhausted Mary, "all of the other interviewers have already asked me that same question. I'm sure that they, along with what is in my résumé, can give you all the background information you need about me. Can we just get to the meat of the interview? I've been here all day and I'm really tired."

The interviewer seemed startled by Mary's response, and she noticed that he made a brief note to himself. *I guess he probably wasn't thrilled with that,* she thought to herself, *but enough is enough.* Within fifteen minutes, however, the fifth interview was completed and the interviewer had politely excused himself. *Oh well,* thought Mary, *I'm pretty sure that I made a good impression on all of the other interviewers I've talked with so far.*

ARRIVING FOR YOUR INTERVIEW

As we discussed in Chapter 8, the most important thing that you can do to start off on the right foot is to arrive for your interview a few minutes early. This demonstrates to the interviewer that you are punctual and truly interested in the job. It also provides you with a few minutes to catch your breath before the interview begins. In general, arriving about ten to fifteen minutes early is perceived positively. Arriving late is a huge error that could cost you the job before the interview even begins.

Be aware of how you interact with everyone you meet from the moment you walk in the door. From the receptionist at the front desk to the interviewers and managers with whom you may meet, treat everyone with complete courtesy and respect. I've been told repeatedly by receptionists and administrative assistants that their opinions are frequently asked about interview candidates. Being rude to a receptionist is a surefire way to get off to a bad start.

THE INTERVIEW AS A TWO-WAY PROCESS

All too many job seekers view the interview as a one-way road. *The interviewer is going to ask me a bunch of questions and I need to answer them to the best of my ability,* they think. You certainly do need to answer the questions well, but this is also your opportunity to decide whether the job and the organization are right for you. With some careful observations and questioning, you can make a much more informed decision if and when the job is offered to you.

Observe everything, from the moment you walk in the door. By arriving a few minutes early for your interview, you'll have more time to look around and get a feel for the climate within the organization. Do people seem happy, or are they rushing around with scowling faces? Are they chatting with each other? Does the atmosphere seem relaxed, or do you sense a lot of pressure? You can tell a lot about an organization's culture just from spending a few minutes there.

One job seeker arrived for his interview at the offices of a large trade association and was escorted to a reception area to wait for a few minutes. As he watched people walk back and forth through the reception area, he observed that they moved like robots—very quickly, with total seriousness and with little interpersonal interaction when they passed. The job seeker also observed that the receptionist, while crisp and efficient, demonstrated no warmth to anyone passing by.

He filed this away as something to think about. At the end of his interview, he decided to ask about corporate culture. "What is the corporate culture here like?" he asked. "What is it like to work here?" After a slight pause, the interviewer pulled out a sheet of paper and proceeded to draw and explain the details of an organizational chart. The question asked by the candidate was totally ignored. The job was offered to the job seeker a few days later. The salary and benefits were good, and the job itself was a good fit. The job seeker, however, turned it down. Based on his observations and the way his question about corporate culture had been handled, he didn't feel the organization would be a pleasant place to work. He didn't want to again be looking for a job in six months because he was unhappy.

STRUCTURE OF AN INTERVIEW

Most interview candidates don't understand that a good interview doesn't just happen. A productive interview actually has a structure. To be effective, all questions must be planned and well thought out. This is the only way for the interviewer to ensure that he or she gets the information needed about you. As an interview candidate, it helps to understand the structure of a typical interview in order to best be prepared to handle it.

So what does a typical interview structure look like? The percentages are approximate, but one typical structure looks like this:

Opening/Icebreaker (5 Percent)

Believe it or not, most interviewers do want you to be successful. If you are successful in conveying your skills and interests, they can do the best possible job of making a hiring decision. When they make a good hiring decision, they look good too.

The best way for an interviewer to help you be successful is to try to make you comfortable and at ease. For that reason, most interviewers will open the interview with some "small talk" or an icebreaker question to reduce the tension. This is not an invitation to you to totally relax. You must still maintain your professionalism and composure, but it is an effort to reduce the butterflies in your stomach. If you are interviewing for a position that requires a lot of interpersonal contact, how well you handle this conversation could also become part of the evaluation process.

Job/Organizational Culture (10 Percent)

You probably received at least a general description of the job for which you are interviewing, and you may have also received information about the company in advance. Many recruiters, however, will take the time to tell you a little bit more about the position, the department in which it resides, and the organization in general. They want you to have as clear a view as possible of what you are getting into. Both of you will eventually need to make a decision about whether the job and the culture are a good fit for you.

Listen carefully if more information is offered. Although taking copious notes during an interview isn't recommended, do feel free to jot down any key facts you want to remember. Also make note of any questions that come to mind as the additional information is offered. If you don't have the opportunity to ask questions during this part of the interview, one of these questions may be a good to ask later at the end of the interview.

Questioning/Information Gathering (75 Percent)

You will be in the spotlight for the bulk of the interview. A good recruiter will let you do most of the talking so that he or she can find out as much as possible about you, your background, and your skills. During this questioning/information gathering, you can expect a combination of some of the traditional interview questions covered in the previous chapter (especially if the interview is an initial screening) and more complex questions related to your profession. You should be ready for both.

Your answers should be both thorough and concise. The time available for the interview is probably limited, but the interviewer needs to learn as much about you and your skills as possible. Try to answer the questions asked as directly as possible. Be sure to include specific examples showing how you have displayed the behaviors or used the skills being discussed in the past. Your specific evidence lends credibility to your answers.

Candidate Questions (5 Percent)

Most interviewers leave a little time at the end of the interview for any questions that you may have. Don't expect time for an extensive discussion or answers to a long list of questions, but do be prepared with at least a couple of questions you would like answered. Not having any questions could send an unintentional message that you aren't all that interested in the job. The common interview questions in Chapter 8 include several questions you might consider using, but you may also have questions that come directly out of the discussion that has taken place during the interview.

Wrap-Up/Next Steps (5 Percent)

At the very end of the interview, your interviewer should give you an idea of what the next steps in the process will be and what the time line will be. If that information isn't offered, be sure to ask! You need to know the time line so that you can decide when and how it is appropriate to follow up if you don't hear anything.

In general, remember that a good interviewer will be prepared with some sort of interview structure and questions. The interviewer needs to maintain control of the interview in order to learn those things about you most critical to the hiring decision and will need to move the interview along to fit the available time constraints. Be sure that you do everything you can to help in that endeavor by being well prepared, providing thorough but concise answers to questions, and staying on track.

THE SILENT INTERVIEW

Just as important as the "actual" interview—the questions asked and answered—is the "silent" interview. How you comport yourself during your interview can either enhance what you say or totally detract from the quality of your answers. Be sure that everything you do supports the words that come out of your mouth.

Your Body Language

One of the biggest initial impressions you make is with your handshake. Most interviewers respond positively to a firm, confident handshake. A handshake says a great deal about your confidence in yourself in a stressful situation.

Eye contact is also extremely important, both in your initial impression and throughout the interview. Making confident and sustained eye contact with everyone you meet, and particularly with the interviewer, sends a strong message about your level of self-confidence. Candidates unsure about their skills or lacking self-confidence often betray their unease by staring at the floor. A good interviewer will quickly pick up on that. Of course, you don't want to start a staring contest, but you should maintain a good level of eye contact with every interviewer both to build rapport and to project your faith in yourself.

One recruiter I know told me about an interview wherein the candidate looked over his head and out the window the entire time. Although the candidate avoided the error of staring at the floor, he was still unable to maintain any kind of eye contact with the interviewer. He came across as being unsure of himself—or, worse, uninterested in the job—and was not invited back for a second interview.

You should also be aware of your posture, both while standing and while seated. If the stress of the interview situation makes you ill at ease, you may convey that unconsciously by slouching. Stand erect and walk confidently. When seated, sit upright and lean forward slightly to convey your interest and enthusiasm in what is being discussed.

Resist the urge to fidget or play with your jewelry, a pen, or any other object. Although a certain amount of nervousness is to be expected when you are going through the interview process, fidgeting can distract the interviewer from fully listening to your answers to the interview questions. One recruiter reported that a candidate fidgeted with her necklace until it was wound so tightly around one of her fingers that it was caught! The interruption and embarrassment detracted from the quality of the interview.

Finally, your body language should convey an energetic nature. In a tough economic environment, employers want to hire candidates with vigor who will be able to hit the ground running. A candidate who is too laid-back or lethargic runs the risk of being perceived as lacking the enthusiasm necessary to excel at the job. Of course you want to appear relaxed, if possible, rather than nervous, but don't overdo it.

Your Voice and Tone

It may sound funny to include voice and tone in our discussion of the "silent" interview, but we do so because while you may not give them much thought, your voice and tone convey a great deal to the interviewer. The most common issues are speaking too quietly or mumbling your answers. Not only does this convey a lack of confidence, but in extreme situations interviewers report struggling just to hear what candidates are saying—not encouraging, since you're supposed to be making it easier for them!

Another common issue is a candidate whose voice lacks any real inflection, speaking in a monotone. Some of us have voices that don't naturally have a lot of inflection, and this can be difficult to overcome. A monotonous voice suggests a lack of interest, however, and that can impact the impression you make on an interviewer. You may need to practice conveying more enthusiasm in your voice.

One good way to check your vocal quality is to call your own voicemail and leave an extended message. When you listen to the message, ask yourself these questions:

○ Am I loud enough? Can I easily hear what I am saying in the message?
○ Does my voice sound confident?
○ Is there enough inflection in my voice?

Also be aware of whether you have a tendency to "trail off" at the end of sentences. You may start your sentences with good volume and inflection, but by the end of the sentence your voice lowers and disappears. This gives a distinct impression that you really aren't confident about what you are saying and potentially not secure in your knowledge of the subject at hand.

Finally, beware of ending your sentences with a "verbal question mark"—signified by a rising inflection at the end of each sentence. Some people have a speech pattern that naturally ends with what sounds like a question. Again, this gives an air of insecurity to the answer. Any of these problems should be apparent from the voicemail exercise. You can also ask a trusted friend to give you an honest assessment of any speech patterns you have that may be problematic.

TYPES OF INTERVIEWS

The various types of interviews call for diverse strategies. Each interview type has advantages and disadvantages for both the interviewer and the candidate. You'll probably encounter each of the types of interviews described below during the course of your job search. Understanding both the advantages and disadvantages for you as a candidate will help you better strategize for success.

Telephone Interviews

Telephone interviews are generally used due to constraints of time, distance, or money. They are among the most common interview methods for initial screenings because of the time and money that they save. However, they can also be useful in situations where people in a variety of geographic locations need to interview the candidate, or for some reason the candidate is not able to travel to the interview site.

Advantages of Telephone Interviews
- You interview in your own comfortable environment.
- There are fewer logistical concerns.
- They eliminate distance/travel issues.

Disadvantages of Telephone Interviews
- It's more difficult to build rapport with the interviewer(s).
- You may be unprepared for the call.

Telephone Interview Tips
1. **Dress for the interview, even though they can't see you.** Wearing your pajamas and fuzzy slippers may seem like a good idea to make you as comfortable as possible, but you won't feel or sound as professional. Dressing in at least business casual clothing sends a message to your brain that this is serious!
2. **Be aware of the tone and inflection of your voice.** Because the interviewer has no visual cues to go by, your voice takes on even more importance. Beware of sounding bored or distracted, or speaking with a monotone. You may have the best qualifications in the world, but if you sound uninterested or unenthusiastic, it could cripple your chances.
3. **If the interviewer calls without warning and the timing isn't good, say so.** Ask whether you can speak with the interviewer at a time that is more suitable. Speaking too softly because colleagues are nearby or shouting over a dog barking in the background won't inspire confidence. Better to have the conversation when you can concentrate on the questions appropriately and present yourself in the best possible way.
4. **Have water nearby to sip if you need it.** Many people find telephone interviews to be stressful, and as a result their mouths dry out and their voices crack, betraying nervousness.

An occasional sip of water will help maintain the quality of your voice.

Panel Interviews

Panel interviews are commonly used when several people need to interview the same candidate. The typical format is several people gathered around a conference table with the candidate at one end. All the interviewers share the role of asking the candidate questions. Although efficient and a time-saver for the employer, many candidates find panel interviews to be either intimidating or downright scary.

Advantages of Panel Interviews
○ They save time for both you and the interviewers.
○ Multiple interviewers can hear and evaluate the same answers to the same questions.
○ They provide consistency among the candidates (if each interviewer asks similar questions of you).
○ You have the opportunity to see how panel members interact with each other, which can provide insight into their corporate culture.

Disadvantages of Panel Interviews
○ These interviews are almost always more intimidating for the candidate.
○ One or two interviewers may dominate the questioning.
○ It is more difficult to build rapport with multiple interviewers.
○ You have to put forth substantially more effort in your follow-up.

Panel Interview Tips
1. **Address your answers, one at a time, to the specific interviewer who asked the question.** In most scenarios, each interviewer will ask at least one question, and this will

give you a brief chance to connect with each member of the panel.

2. **Do not ignore any of the panel members.** One candidate worked hard to build rapport with the male members of a panel (assuming that this was where the power was) and virtually ignored the female members. The female CEO quickly dismissed him as a viable candidate.

3. **Be sure to follow up with all panel members.** Attempt to get a business card from each person.

Serial (One-on-One) Interviews

A series of consecutive one-on-one, or *serial*, interviews is probably the most common corporate interviewing format. A candidate is brought in for several hours or a day and interviewed in succession by several interviewers. A "host" interviewer generally starts and finishes the day with the candidate to provide continuity. That person is typically also the point person for your follow-up.

Serial interviews may include some sort of "downtime," such as lunch. You will likely be told something like "you can relax now, we're just going to have a casual lunch." Don't buy it! Whether the interviewer(s) realize it or not, they will continue to subconsciously evaluate you during the "downtime." You should expect to continue to do most of the talking, even in this casual setting. Order food that will be easy to eat, and abstain from alcoholic beverages.

Advantages of Serial Interviews

○ Typically these are less intimidating for the candidate because of the one-on-one format.

○ Both you and the interviewer have the opportunity to interact and build rapport.

○ They are easier for both you and the interviewer to pursue follow-up questions.

Disadvantages of Serial Interviews

○ They can be exhausting for you if they extend through an entire day.
○ If not well coordinated, you may be asked the same questions repeatedly.
○ They are more time consuming—you may have to devote an entire half-day or day to the process.

Serial Interview Tips

1. Be well rested so that you can maintain your energy and enthusiasm during a potentially long day.
2. Be prepared to answer the same question(s) more than once, maintaining your enthusiasm each time.

BEHAVIORAL INTERVIEWING

Regardless of the type of interview used, many employers have in recent years started using a technique called *behavioral interviewing*. The technique is based on the premise that the best indicator of future behavior is past behavior. In other words, if you were able to successfully address a situation in the past, you likely will be able to successfully handle a similar situation in the future.

Behavioral interview questions typically include a cue that prompts you to offer a specific real-life example. For instance, many behavioral questions begin with words like "Tell me about a time . . ." or "Think back to a time when . . ." Those signals should tell you that you need to review your previous experiences and come up with a very specific example of the behavior or action involved. Some employers will even explain to you up front that they use behavioral interviewing and stress the importance of you giving very specific examples from your background in your answers.

The best way to prepare for possible behavioral interview questions is, again, to take a careful look at the job description for the position for which you will be interviewing. What are the key skills that are emphasized? If the employer uses behavioral interviewing (and most do to at least some extent), these are the skill sets you will likely be asked about. Think about and practice specific examples related to these skills ahead of time, and you'll be much better prepared if behavioral questions are asked.

The following is a list of common behavioral interview questions, sorted by competency. Studying them should give you a good idea of the general direction these questions take.

Behavioral Interviewing: Common Topic Areas and Typical Questions

COMPETENCY: CLIENT SERVICE

- Tell me about a time when a client came to you angry (although not necessarily at you). How did you work with the client to resolve the issue?
- Describe a situation in which you went the extra mile to please a client.
- Tell me about a time when you delighted a client. How did you know that you did?

COMPETENCY: INTERPERSONAL SKILLS

- Think back to a situation in which you were involved in a conflict. What did you do to resolve the conflict?
- Describe a project on which you were the team leader. How did you work with and motivate your team to complete the project successfully?
- Describe a situation in which you had to tell your boss some very bad news.

COMPETENCY: SELF-MANAGEMENT

- Tell me about a professional risk you took. What was the outcome?
- Describe a learning opportunity you pursued to increase your professional knowledge.
- Tell me about an important goal you had to set and how you met that goal.

COMPETENCY: CHANGE MANAGEMENT

- Describe a time when you had to lead your team through a major change. How did you manage the team members' adjustment to the change?
- Tell me about the most difficult work-related change you've been through. What was your role, and what specific steps did you take to succeed?

SECOND INTERVIEWS

Most employers won't make a decision based on just one interview. The first interview is typically a "screening interview." A large number of applicants who have good-looking credentials on paper are granted an initial interview (either in person or by phone), and from that group a few finalists are usually chosen. The first interview is really a "make it or break it" step for continuing with the process.

If you are called back for a second interview, it almost always means that you are one of a handful of finalists. In many cases it also means that the key decision maker(s) have not yet gotten involved in the process (especially if the human resources department conducted the initial screening). Your competition (the other finalists) will probably also be very well qualified. You must approach the second interview with the same enthusiasm, knowledge base, and level of preparedness as you did the first interview. This is when things really get serious!

Some employers will even extend the process beyond a second interview, particularly if the position is a fairly high-level one. Some applicants get irritated when this happens and begin to wonder if the employer is just stringing them along. Don't do this—keep in mind that the employer wants to make the best possible decision about who the best "fit" is for the job. Hiring mistakes are expensive, and starting the process again can take months. Be patient, even if the process does drag on through several levels of interviewing.

WHAT DO YOU DO ABOUT INAPPROPRIATE/ILLEGAL INTERVIEW QUESTIONS?

Most interviewers have been well trained and understand that interview questions shouldn't violate Equal Employment

Opportunity policy or the Americans with Disabilities Act. Some interviewers, however—especially line managers who may be asked to participate in the interview process for a specific position, but don't regularly interview candidates—haven't been well trained and aren't aware of what they should or shouldn't ask. You may find yourself in a situation where you are asked a question that is inappropriate and that you prefer not to answer. You'll need to decide on the spot how to most effectively handle the situation.

The line between legal and illegal questions is often unclear. In general, questions not directly related to the responsibilities of the position and your qualifications are not legal. Questions may also be technically legal but not appropriate. Among the types of questions that you should not be asked are those about:

○ Age
○ Nationality
○ Race
○ Marital status
○ Children or number of children
○ Sexual orientation
○ Religion

This list isn't exhaustive, but it gives you an idea of the types of things you shouldn't be asked.

If you do find yourself being asked something that you perceive as either illegal or inappropriate, you have decide quickly how to handle it. Part of that decision may be based on your assessment of the interviewer and the intent with which you think the question was asked. Do you think that the interviewer is intentionally looking for information that will affect his or her decision, or is the person innocently not aware that the question is illegal or inappropriate? (For instance, an unknowing interviewer might ask about your children in the course of casual opening chitchat.) You have three possible courses of action:

○ You find the question (and possibly the intent) so offensive that you decide not to continue with the interview. You politely end the interview and leave.

○ You don't want to answer the question, but you want to continue with the interview process. You can respectfully decline to answer the question ("I don't think that information is really relevant to my qualifications for this position") and ask to move on to the next question.

○ You don't feel that answering the question will impact you negatively, and knowing that it is illegal or inappropriate, you decide to answer anyway.

One of my clients was interviewing for a fairly high-level management position that required traveling up to 50 percent of the time (as clearly stated in the job description). When she interviewed for the job, she was confronted with questions about whether or not she was married and whether she had children. She really was interested in the job, so she responded that she was and that she had three children. The invasive questioning continued, with questions about whether her husband traveled for his job and whether she had adequate child care arrangements. At this point my client became irritated and realized that this wasn't the kind of organization or environment in which she wanted to work. She politely excused herself and ended the interview.

The employer in this situation was obviously concerned about the ability of applicants to travel. Perhaps they had been burned in the past by employees who said they could travel when interviewed, but then couldn't when they actually got hired. Because the travel requirement was written in the job description, the employer could have certainly asked something like this: "The requirements for this job include the ability to travel up to 50 percent of the time. Are you able to fulfill this requirement without trouble?"

The approach the employer chose to take instead was at best inappropriate, and possibly illegal. My client's decision to remove herself from the situation and from consideration for the job made sense under the circumstances.

There is no right or wrong strategy if you are faced with a similar situation. You will need to quickly assess what is going on and make the best decision you can about how to handle the questioning. Being forewarned that these sorts of circumstances do happen, however, will better prepare you to handle them.

WHAT ABOUT SALARY QUESTIONS?

It's not at all unusual for salary questions to come up during the course of an interview. Your potential employer may ask what your salary expectations are or what your current salary level is. They legitimately want to know whether they can "afford" you, and whether your expectations are within the range for the job. The salary question is one of the most difficult for applicants to deal with.

Your best approach is to have some data about what reasonable expectations are for the job, the type of organization, and the geographic area. This will require some homework on your part, researching average salary levels. The section on negotiating in Chapter 10 includes a number of resources you can use to do that research. You must remember that salary is *not* about what you want or need! It's about the market value of the job.

If you are asked about salary, try not to be pinned down to a specific figure or appear inflexible. One approach is to have a range in mind based on the research that you have done. You might say something like "It's my understanding based on some research I did that the average range for this type of position would be between $X and $Y. I would like to find myself somewhere in that range." That approach tells an employer that you've done your homework and have an idea what the market range for the job is. Because you mention a range rather than a specific figure, you display some flexibility in your expectations.

Being asked about your current or most recent salary can be a real challenge. If your most recent salary was significantly below what you feel the job you are interviewing is worth (based on your research), mention the research and that you feel you were somewhat underpaid compared to the market. If you were significantly overpaid and don't think this employer will match your previous salary, again, go back to your research. Also mention that you understand that the learning curve in a new company or industry might reduce your value a bit from what you were being paid. Either way, you show a knowledge of your value, and that it isn't necessarily tied to your previous salary.

INTERVIEW MELTDOWN: WHAT DO YOU DO IF . . .

○ **. . . a question is asked, and you need time to think about the answer?** Regardless of how well you prepare, you will likely encounter at least a few questions that you aren't totally prepared for. You may need a few seconds just to think. As uncomfortable as the silence may be, take those few seconds to really consider the best answer. You may even say something like "let me just take a moment to think about that question." This approach will give you time to formulate a much better answer than just blurting out the first thing that comes to your mind.

You may also find that you don't understand the question. Rather than answering the question you think you heard, and possibly getting it wrong, you can always verify with the interviewer exactly what is being asked. Paraphrasing is a very effective tool to use here. You might say something like "What I think I hear you asking is . . . ," and state the question as you understood it. The interviewer will either verify that you understand the question correctly or will rephrase to make it clearer.

If you draw a complete blank when asked a question, you may feel yourself starting to panic. Although it's not ideal, you may need to ask the interviewer to move on to the next question and return to the difficult question a few minutes later. It's not a perfect resolution to the situation, but it is far better than saying the first thing that comes to mind.

○   **. . . the interviewer does all the talking?** Although most human resources people receive at least some interview training, many line managers don't. If you make it to the second stage of the interviewing process, you'll likely be interviewing with your future supervisor and/or your future peers. If they lack any training in how to conduct an interview, they may be as nervous as you are. This nervousness may manifest itself in them rambling on and doing most of the talking. You may not have a chance to really present yourself or your skills.

In this type of scenario, you may need to gracefully assume some control. Even a "motor mouth" will need to take a breath at some point, and you may need to jump in. If you've researched the job description thoroughly and you understand some of the key skill sets, you might try saying something like "I understand that this skill is essential to being able to do this job well. I'd like to share a couple of examples with you of how I've developed and used this skill in the past." Your untrained interviewer may actually be relieved to sit back for a few minutes and listen.

○   **. . . you forget to make a key point in answering one of the interviewer's questions?** The close of the interview is an opportunity to tie up any loose ends. Most interviewers will ask whether you have anything additional to share, and this is your opportunity to expand on anything that you may have forgotten.

Alternatively, you may suddenly remember as you are driving home from the interview an important point you forgot to make. Your thank-you letter is an ideal opportunity to briefly outline what you forgot to say.

In either case, be sure to follow up in some way with the missing information. It could make the difference between you getting or not getting the job!

ENDING THE INTERVIEW: CLOSE THE SALE!

As the interview comes to an end, you will have an opportunity to make a final impression. Just as your first impression is critical, your final impression will be too. Anything positive that happened during the interview may be lost if your final impression overshadows it.

The final moments of the interview are your opportunity to "close the sale," which is critical in a tough economy. Most of your competitors will merely shake the interviewer's hand, say thank you, and leave the room. But if you truly are interested in the job, you should say so! Confidently tell the interviewer that you are very excited about what you have heard during the interview and you want him or her to know you are very interested and want the job. The message delivered is that you are confident in your qualifications and you truly have a strong interest.

You must also be sure that you have all the information you need regarding the next steps in the process, and what the employer's time line is to make a decision. Most interviewers will volunteer this information as they close the interview. If they don't, ask! You need to know whether there is another step in the interview process, and when you might be called back. Knowing the time line will help you decide at what point it is appropriate to follow up if you haven't heard anything.

To properly follow up, you need to be sure that you have sufficient contact information for everyone who interviewed you. Ask for business cards if at all possible. A business card will give you the correct spelling of everyone's name, a direct phone number, and e-mail and mailing addresses for your thank you.

As you leave the interview, remember to show the same courtesies you did when you arrived. Be sure to thank everyone for their hospitality (including the receptionist and any administrative people who have assisted you). That way, anyone asked for an opinion will have a favorable impression of his or her interaction with you.

INTERVIEW HORROR STORIES

Every recruiter has a favorite horror story about a candidate who totally blew the interview and was oblivious as to why. Here are a couple of my favorite real-life stories. Consider yourself armed!

- **Is it time for lunch?** A recruiting manager for a consulting firm in northern Virginia shared this story with me. A candidate arrived for an early afternoon interview. As he entered the recruiting manager's office, he pulled out a fast food bag from a popular chain restaurant. "I didn't get a chance to have lunch yet," he said. "Do you mind if I eat while we talk?" Without waiting for an answer from the recruiter, he proceeded to move several items on her desk to make way for him to spread out his lunch. Needless to say, the interview was short.

- **Help from Mom.** A recruiter in Washington, D.C., recounted the story of a recent college graduate who arrived for an interview. The young woman was accompanied by her mother, and much to the surprise of the recruiter, the mother followed into the office when it was time for the interview. As the recruiter started the interview, the mother interrupted the candidate and began to answer the interviewer's questions. Even when the recruiter tried to ignore the mother and address the candidate, the behavior continued. Another interview cut short, with hugely negative consequences for the candidate!

- **Ignore half the interview panel.** A candidate for a position at a nonprofit organization was interviewed by a panel of four people. Two were men and two were women. Throughout the interview, the candidate focused his attention only on the men on the panel. All of his eye contact and body language focused only on the male interviewers. Even when the women on the panel asked him questions, his answers were directed at the men. After the candidate left, the women were irate. Based on his "silent interview" signals, he had destroyed any chance of being hired.

---○---

KEVIN'S INTERVIEW

Kevin had been interviewing for a new position for the past hour. He felt that the interview had gone well, that he had answered the various questions effectively, and that he had built a good rapport with the interviewer. He was very interested in the job but knew that the competition for the position would be stiff. As the interview neared an end, Kevin knew he needed to do something to stand out (in a positive way) with the interviewer.

The interviewer completed the questioning and told Kevin about the next steps in the process.

"Thanks for coming in today," said the interviewer. "I appreciate the opportunity to learn more about you and your qualifications for this position."

"Thank you," said Kevin. "I'm glad to have the opportunity to talk with you. I want you to know that I'm really excited about what you've told me today about this position and about your organization. I'm very interested in this job, and I truly believe that I am the best candidate you will find."

Wow, thought the recruiter. *That's quite assertive, but it sure does tell me that he really wants this job and is convinced that he can do it well. No one else has really said that in the same way.*

Kevin left the interview feeling confident that he had done the best possible job in presenting himself and his qualifications. He would follow up immediately while the interview was still fresh in the recruiter's mind.

---○---

After any interview, it's a good idea to complete a debriefing document of your own, to sort your thoughts about how the interview went and possibly see what could be improved in the future. It's important that you are as honest and objective as possible in filling out this document; otherwise it won't be much use. See the sample format in Worksheet 9.1 at the end of this chapter.

This can also help you keep track of the people you've heard from, those you need to send thank yous to, and those you may need to follow up with. If you feel comfortable enough doing it, you can also show these to your job search buddy, who may find them helpful in getting a sense of how your search is going and how he or she might be able to help.

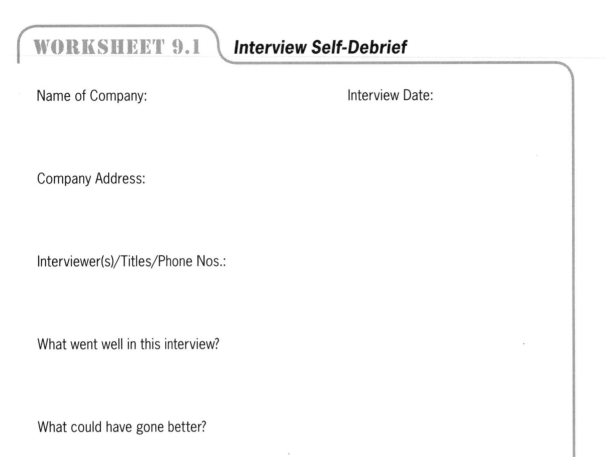

WORKSHEET 9.1 *Interview Self-Debrief*

Name of Company: Interview Date:

Company Address:

Interviewer(s)/Titles/Phone Nos.:

What went well in this interview?

What could have gone better?

Information you forgot to provide in your answers:

Additional materials you need to provide to the employer:

Thank you sent and date:

WORKSHEET 9.1

Name of Company: Interview Date:

Company Address:

Interviewer(s)/Titles/Phone Nos.

What went well in this interview?

What could have gone better?

Information you forgot to provide in your answers:

Additional materials you need to provide to the employer:

Thank you sent and date:

Following Up

How to Stand Out and Clinch the Deal

Many candidates don't realize that what they do *after* the interview can have almost as great an impact as what they do *during* the interview. Not following up appropriately (or not following up at all) can deliver a variety of messages to the recruiter: that you don't care, you don't see things through, or you don't understand the importance of social niceties in the business world.

For Sharon, a director in a fundraising firm, these concerns were way too important to ignore. She interviewed a candidate whom she considered perfect for her open fundraising position. The candidate interviewed extremely well, was personable, and appeared to have all the skills and qualifications to do a great job. In the days following the interview, Sharon waited for some kind of follow-up from the candidate. She had already spoken to the human resources contact, and the job offer was ready. Sharon had decided that she would make the offer as soon as the candidate followed up. No thank-you letter, phone call, or any other follow-up ever occurred. Sharon didn't make the offer, reasoning that a total lack of follow-up after the interview would translate to lack of follow-up with clients.

---⊙---

MARY'S FOLLOW-UP

Several weeks had passed since Mary's interview. She felt that the meeting had gone well and that she had been able to build a good rapport with the interviewer. At the end of the interview, she had conveyed her strong interest in the job. She also had followed up with a short thank-you letter the very next day. In short, she felt that she had done everything correctly in this phase of her job search process.

Despite her efforts, however, she had heard nothing from the employer. She had been told that a final decision would be made within three weeks, but more than six weeks had now passed. Mary was feeling frustrated, and that frustration was turning into anger. How dare they leave her hanging for such a long time!

Finally, Mary decided that she needed to find out what was going on. She picked up the phone to call Sylvia, who had led the team of interviewers. After a couple of voicemail messages back and forth, Mary had really worked herself into an agitated state. When she finally got Sylvia on the other end of the phone, a tense exchange took place.

"Hello, Sylvia," said Mary. "I interviewed with you more than six weeks ago for what sounded like a great opportunity. I thought that I interviewed well and that we had built a good rapport. You told me that you would be making a decision within three weeks, and more than six weeks have now gone by. What the heck is going on with you people down there? How long are you going to keep me waiting?"

Sylvia listened on the other end of the phone in stunned silence. For the past month she had been dealing with the aftermath of her husband's serious heart attack. Several work projects had been delayed as she faced this major personal crisis, and completing the hiring process for this position had been one of them.

"I'm so sorry, Mary," said Sylvia. "There has been a lot going on here, and several things have been delayed. We just haven't been able to complete the hiring process for the position you interviewed for. We hope to make a decision and an offer fairly soon, but I can't give you a specific time line."

Excuses, excuses, thought Mary. "Well fine," she answered. "Just understand that I may be receiving other offers soon, and I can't be waiting around for you people to make up your minds." With that,

Mary hung up the phone. *Good,* she thought to herself. *I've put some pressure on them to get this process moving.*

Sylvia hung up the phone slowly. *That was pretty aggressive,* she thought. *We liked Mary's qualifications, and we were really considering her as a finalist, but after that exchange I think we had better reconsider!*

HOW SHOULD YOUR THANK YOU BE HANDLED?

You should plan to follow up on your interview with some sort of thank you. Some career professionals disagree as to whether the thank you should be in the form of an e-mail message or a more traditional hard-copy letter.

The best advice is to consider the type of organization at which you interviewed and its culture. An interviewer at an innovative high-tech organization will probably respond best to an e-mail message. One recruiter at an Internet consulting firm recently told me that they secretly laughed about candidates who followed up with a hard-copy thank-you letter or note. They reasoned that if the follow-up didn't happen electronically, the candidate might not be comfortable with a high-tech culture. Another reason to use e-mail is if there is a time constraint that demands the interviewer see your thank you immediately.

If you interviewed at a more traditional organization, a hard-copy letter will probably be a better bet. A bank executive shared with me that he expects candidates to send a professional hard-copy thank-you letter. He is offended if he receives anything less. In either case, a thank you shows good follow-up on your part and could set you apart from the competition.

If you send a hard-copy letter, the other question is whether it should be handwritten or typed. If your handwriting is poor, the answer is simple—send a typed letter. A handwritten letter is acceptable only if it is neatly written on professional business stationery. Don't make the mistake of one candidate I once interviewed, who sent a handwritten thank-you note on stationery adorned with cute pictures of kittens.

Your thank-you message doesn't have to be elaborate. It should, however, be professional and businesslike. An effective thank-you letter or e-mail can be as few as three paragraphs. One possible format for a thank-you letter follows:

○ **Paragraph one:** Tell the interviewer that you appreciated the opportunity to interview for the position. Thank him or her for extending it.
○ **Paragraph two:** Refer back to something discussed during the interview. During your interview, did you forget to mention an example of how you displayed or used a key skill in the past? This is the place to refer back to that part of the interview and mention your example. If you didn't forget anything, refer back to a couple of portions of the interview discussion that you found particularly interesting, or where you felt you made a good impression.
○ **Paragraph three:** Thank the interviewer again. If you will be following up in some way, mention the follow-up and when the interviewer can expect to hear from you. If you do say in your thank-you letter that you will follow up, you absolutely must do so, in accordance with the time line you mentioned.

A sample thank-you letter is shown in Worksheet 10.1 at the end of this chapter. This is a fairly safe format that should be acceptable in any industry or company culture.

WHAT IF YOU DON'T HEAR ANYTHING?

Most interviewers will give you some idea of when you can expect to get feedback about the status of your candidacy. The flip side, however, is that they often don't live up to the promises they make. Whether because of conflicting priorities or undue optimism about when they will be able to deliver, you often won't hear from the interviewer within the promised time line.

If this happens, don't despair! You don't know what else has gotten in the way of making a decision. Often unforeseen projects have come up or key decision makers are out of the office. If you have the interviewer's phone number, give him or her a call. In a nonthreatening way, tell that person you are just calling to follow up because he or she had told you a decision would be made in about this timeframe. Say that you are still very interested in the job and ask whether a decision has been reached yet. The answer will often be that it hasn't, but sometimes the answer is the job has been offered to someone else. Be prepared to accept the latter response gracefully. Knowing that the job has been offered to someone else is better than not knowing anything.

WHAT SHOULD YOU DO IF YOU GET THE OFFER?

Congratulations when you land that elusive job offer! Just because you've gotten an offer, however, your work is not done. You need to carefully consider the elements of any job offer you receive.

Don't Accept on the Spot

Any ethical organization is going to understand that you need time to evaluate the offer. At the very least, you should take a minimum of a couple of days to evaluate all aspects of the offer. After all, this is a huge decision with a big impact on your life and your future. You may also have a spouse or significant other with whom you need to discuss the offer and what it will mean for both of you. If you are pressured to accept on the spot, be suspicious. The organization may be trying to "lowball" you and not want to give you adequate time to think about the offer and do some research.

Ask for the Offer in Writing

The first offer you get may very well be verbal, but be sure that you get an offer in writing. It's critical that both you and the employer have exactly the same understanding of all of the elements of the offer, and this can be confusing if everything is done verbally. Having everything in writing protects both you and the employer.

One candidate accepted a verbal offer in which he was given a week more vacation than was usually given to new employees. This was partly to compensate for a salary that was a little less than the market standard. He arrived for his first day of work to find that the person who had made him the offer was no longer with the organization. No one else knew about some unique aspects of the offer, including the extra week of vacation, and he had no proof. Fortunately, the person who had made him the offer had left the organization on good terms, and when contacted was able to confirm what the candidate had been offered. However, the candidate could easily have been stripped of the extra week and still earning below-market salary. Problems such as these can be alleviated with a written offer.

CAN YOU NEGOTIATE WITH YOUR POTENTIAL EMPLOYER?

In many cases, that first offer from the employer won't be totally acceptable to you. After doing your market research, you really feel that you are worth more than the salary being offered. Or perhaps the benefit package isn't quite what you expected. You may very well find yourself in a situation where you want to negotiate some aspects of the offer you have received.

Know the "Market Value" of the Job

Before you even think about negotiating salary, you need to know the "market value" of the job you've been offered. In other words, for that type of job, in that geographic area, for that type and size employer, what is the job you've been offered really worth? Many job hunters have unrealistic expectations of the salary they will be offered based primarily on personal needs and wants.

To find out market value, you need to find out what similar jobs of the same type and level are paying in the same geographic area. Geographic area is important because the market value for the same job may vary widely between geographic areas depending on population, cost of living, how hard the job is to fill, and a variety of other pertinent factors. A job in Topeka, Kansas, probably won't have as high a market value as the same job in San Francisco, California.

One place to start looking for salary data is with professional organizations. Many of the major associations conduct annual salary surveys of their membership. They do the surveys both as a service to their members and to document salary trends in the career field or industry they represent. The data are analyzed and published in a variety of ways, including by job title, geographic region, size of company, and so on.

The very best source of salary data is from people who actually work in the field. If in your network you have colleagues working in positions similar to the position you've been offered, survey them about what they see as average salary ranges. You won't want to ask them specifically what their salary levels are, but rather what they see as averages or ranges. They will, however, certainly compute their own salaries into what they tell you, which will provide you with a fairly accurate idea of market value.

Another resource is the U.S. Department of Labor Bureau of Labor Statistics. It collects a wide range of salary data, and slice, dice, and publish the data in a variety of ways. Their website is bls.gov/bls/blswage.htm. The only proviso is that it takes the government a long time to collect and publish the data, so the data may be somewhat outdated, especially in industries known to change quickly, like information technology.

There are also a number of commercial Internet sites that provide a wide range of salary information. Sites such as salary .com and payscale.com allow you to input a range of data about your job title/career field, geographic location, and so on. Be cognizant that data from these sites are gleaned from a variety of sources and can be somewhat outdated or not strictly applicable, depending on the particulars of your situation. Use any salary data you find in conjunction with other salary resources for the most accurate assessment of the "market value" of a position.

Remember That "Negotiate" Is Not a Bad Word

Many people associate the idea of negotiating with the experience of buying a used car—typically not a very pleasant experience. Most organizations will expect there to be some negotiation before a final offer is accepted. You need to go through the negotiating process with a positive, upbeat attitude. Although it may sound trite, the negotiation should end in a "win-win" situation. Both you and the organization need to be comfortable and happy with the final outcome.

Know Your Bottom Line

Have you (and your spouse or partner) actually figured out what your bottom line is to maintain your lifestyle? Do you know how that compares to the market value for your job in your metropolitan area? Are your skills in high demand, or are there many others with the same skills who can do the job? All of these things are important considerations in knowing what your bottom line is. You need to have a concrete idea of what you will and won't accept. In some situations you may have to be prepared to politely walk away if the offer is just too far from what is acceptable.

Things Other Than Salary Are Negotiable!

The offer package is often about much more than salary. Do you need better work-life balance? Perhaps telecommuting and a flexible work schedule are possible options. If you have reached a desired level of vacation accrual with your current employer and wish to maintain it, that benefit might be negotiable (particularly if it is in lieu of a larger salary). Because so many employers have become more cognizant of work-life balance in recent years, many aspects of how, when, and where a job is done have become more negotiable. Especially if the salary level offered is not quite what you anticipated, think about what other parts of the package might be desirable to you.

If salary is an important issue, and there isn't a lot of immediate flexibility in what the employer is willing to offer, you may have another option. Is the employer willing to consider doing a review of your performance after six months of employment instead of one year? Would they be open to negotiation of an additional salary increase at that point? With six months of excellent performance under your belt, the employer will definitely want to keep you!

To help you with your negotiation, two worksheets are offered at the end of this chapter:

○ Worksheet 10.2 will help you to evaluate all of the various aspects of the job offer. Too many job seekers get caught in evaluating only the proposed salary and don't fully take into account the other aspects of the offer.
○ Worksheet 10.3 will help you take a look at your bottom-line living expenses. What sort of salary do you need to maintain your current lifestyle, and does the offer you have received provide adequate compensation?

WHAT IF YOU DON'T GET THE OFFER?

The most important thing to remember if you don't get the job is to not burn your bridges. Certainly, you will be disappointed and probably a little frustrated too. However, you must accept the negative answer with grace and dignity. It's not a direct reflection on you, but rather a case of someone whose qualifications better met the employer's needs. You can take a couple of actions that will leave a favorable impression on the employer.

○ **If you have a phone conversation, be sure to thank the employer for their time and energy in considering you.** Let them know that you are still interested in the organization and would appreciate being considered for any new opportunities that might come up. A phone conversation will also give you the opportunity to find out if there is something you can do to improve your qualifications, or perhaps present them in a different light. You never know what might happen a few weeks or months down the road!

One of my clients understood the concept of following up but didn't quite grasp how to do so *with diplomacy*. When she got the employer on the phone who rejected her, she proceeded to berate him for not hiring her and, after a lengthy tirade, hung up on him. This employer frequently hired my clients, and this woman could conceivably have had another shot in the future. The employer called me, however, and told me never to send that particular client his way again.

In a perfect illustration of the benefits of a polite follow-up, I hired one candidate on his third try. Not only did he react gracefully the first two times, when he wasn't hired, but he had also improved his interview skills each time I met with him. Taking my advice about strengthening his background seriously, he sought out training to improve the skill set that he knew was important to our organization. By the third try he was indeed the ideal candidate for the job—plus, I now had hard evidence of his ability to take advice and follow through.

○ **If there is no phone conversation, consider writing another thank-you note to the employer.** Yes, it probably seems strange to write a thank-you note for being rejected, but thanking the employer for the interviewer's time and energy will leave a favorable impression. There's a good chance none of your competitors will do it, and you'll be favorably regarded for any future openings. In short, you show that you have class.

In any case, don't follow the path of one job hunter I knew! She was both curious and angry about why she didn't get an offer for a position for which she felt she had exceptional qualifications. She called the hiring manager with the intent of simply getting some feedback about how she might have better presented her qualifications. When she got on the phone with the manager, however, her temper got the best of her, and she started to berate him for making the wrong decision. Needless to say, the call was short. Talk about burning bridges! Remember to approach each situation with professionalism, regardless of how unfair you may feel the decision was.

KEVIN'S NEGOTIATION

Kevin had successfully completed the job search process and received an offer for a position he really wanted. He liked what he had learned about the organization, had built a good rapport with his future supervisor, and felt like the job was an ideal fit for his background and skill sets.

The issue was the offer itself. The salary was only a slight increase over his previous job and somewhat under what his research showed to be the market rate. The benefits were acceptable, other than the amount of vacation. He had worked his way up to four weeks of vacation with his previous employer, and this position offered only two weeks for the first two years. Kevin decided that he needed to try to negotiate at least some aspects of the offer. He called Chris, who would be his future boss, to discuss the offer.

"Hi, Chris," said Kevin. "First of all, I want to thank you again for your offer of employment. I really like what I've seen and heard, and I'm very excited about this opportunity. I've been looking at the offer and wanted to talk about a couple parts of it with you. Do you have a few minutes?"

"Sure," answered Chris. *I thought there might be some issues,* he thought. *We don't have a whole lot of room to negotiate with this guy, but he's good and I really don't want to lose him.* "Let's talk about what your concerns are."

This is good, thought Kevin. *At least he is open to talking.* "Well," said Kevin, "I was really hoping that the salary might be a little higher. Based on my research, it's a little below the median for this type of position in this area."

"Agreed," answered Chris. "We knew that when we made the offer. However, we're a pretty small organization, and what we're offering is pretty near the top of what we can afford. I can probably get another $1,000 or $1,500 added on, but that is probably about it. Are there other parts of the offer you want to discuss?"

"Well," answered Kevin, "I also wanted to talk a bit about vacation time. I had worked my way up to four weeks in my previous position and your offer includes two. Is that something we can negotiate on?"

This is an easy fix, thought Chris. *At his level I'm authorized to offer almost what he was getting before.* "Would you be willing to compromise on eighteen total vacation days?" asked Chris. "I can go that high, and it's very close to what you were getting before. If I can do $1,500 more and the extra vacation time, can we move ahead?"

This seems like a good compromise from where we started, thought Kevin. "Okay," said Kevin. "Let's move ahead. I appreciate your flexibility, and I'm really looking forward to a long career with your organization!" The deal was done, and both Kevin and Chris were satisfied with the outcome.

WORKSHEET 10.1 | *Sample Thank-You Letter*

December 12, 2009

Jennifer Jobseeker
123 Main Street
Anywhere, VT 12345

Robert Robertson
Comptroller
XYZ Industries
145 South Street
Somewhere, VT 54321

Dear Mr. Robertson:

Thank you again for the opportunity to meet with you yesterday about the senior accountant position. I was excited by what you shared with me about the position and also with the background information you gave me about XYZ Industries.

As we discussed, my background as a senior staff accountant provides me with strong qualifications for your position. In addition to the many day-to-day responsibilities I hold, I've been instrumental in identifying resources and processes that allow our accounting department to operate with greater efficiency. As you know from our conversation, I've actually been able to lower our operating costs significantly.

I look forward to hearing from you about the senior accountant position. Should you need any additional information about me or have more questions about my background and qualifications, please feel free to contact me. Thank you again for your consideration.

Sincerely,

Jennifer Jobseeker

WORKSHEET 10.2 | *Offer Evaluation*

Use this worksheet to analyze the various components of your job offer. Which of the components are acceptable as is in the offer, and which do you want to try to negotiate?

ITEM	ACCEPTABLE	NEGOTIATE
Salary		
Other compensation (bonus, etc.)		
Benefits (health insurance, etc.)		
Promotion potential		
Career advancement potential		
Vacation		
Sick leave		
Training/education opportunities		
Variety and interest		
Work hours		

WORKSHEET 10.3 \ *Your Bottom Line*

Provide your best estimate of your average monthly expenses in each of the categories below. Add them to come up with your total average monthly financial needs. Multiply times twelve to get your annual financial need. Your annual take-home pay (after taxes) must meet this figure for you to maintain your current lifestyle.

EXPENSE	MONTHLY AVERAGE
Mortgage/rent	
Household maintenance	
Utilities	
Phone/cell phone	
Internet expenses	
Groceries	
Car payments	
Gasoline	
Car maintenance/repairs	
Car insurance	
House insurance	
Health insurance	
Taxes	
Savings	

EXPENSE	MONTHLY AVERAGE
Education	
Child care	
Entertainment	
Health club/gym	
Miscellaneous	
Total Average Monthly Expenses (Total All Above)	.
Total Average Yearly Expenses (Monthly Total × 12)	

Conclusion

I hope you've found this journey helpful! We've examined in detail all of the stages of the job search process—from the preparation you do up front, to the necessity of using a wide variety of strategies, to how you handle the various aspects of the interview. If you follow all of these steps closely, I promise your search will be both shorter and more successful.

I strongly encourage you to read this book more than once so you can truly understand and inhabit the process; you can also use it as a reference whenever you get stuck at a certain stage of the game. The worksheets are here to help, and you should take full advantage of their potential in clarifying and advancing your search. It is not easy to get hired in a tough market. However, I am convinced that people who put in the effort and follow these steps will be the first ones hired—and the most successful in their next positions. Stay positive, and try to view this process as an opportunity to improve your life and advance your career. With this book, your chances of ending up where you want to be—and where you need to be—will be greatly improved.

Best of luck to you on the job search trail!

Index